Dave Elston's passion for spending time in the beautiful Grand Canyon wilderness has produced a series of riveting stories that makes it a must read for anyone who's ever been bitten by the "Canyon Bug." His quest to spend 400 days in "Nature's Grandest Architectural Masterpiece" over a period of years turned him from a green novice into an experienced veteran.

Elston's stories also provide many important lessons in survival. Nature can be very unforgiving. The vicissitudes of the wilderness including the capricious elements, ankle-twisting terrain, a lack of preparation, not understanding one's limitations and a myriad of others have endangered or cost the lives of many who fail to give it proper respect.

This book should be on the shelves of anyone who's ever hiked the challenging trails of the Grand Canyon or ever wanted to.

Marshall Trimble, Arizona State Historian

A Year in the Grand Canyon

Dave Elston

> 10-3-16
> To Lori~
> I really enjoy hiking with your brother, Jim. His name is scattered throughout this book. Hope to meet you some time.
> Dave L. Elston

Vishnu Temple Press

Flagstaff

Copyright © 2016 Dave Elston

First Edition

ISBN 978-0-9905270-8-4

Printed and bound in the United States of America.

All rights reserved.

No part of this book may be reproduced in any form or by any means, including information storage or retrieval systems—except in the case of brief quotations embodied in critical articles or reviews—without written permission from the publisher, Vishnu Temple Press.

Cover painting from an original 2' x 4' original painting, "The North Rim" by Augie Tantalo. Additional Grand Canyon artwork can be viewed at augiesart529@aol.com.

All photographs by Dave Elston unless otherwise attributed.

Vishnu Temple Press
P. O. Box 30821
Flagstaff, Arizona 86003
(928) 556 0742
www.vishnutemplepress.com

A Year in the Grand Canyon

A Collection of Experiences

and Colorful History

from a Lifetime of

Exploring the Grand Canyon

by

Dave Elston

To Jack and Drew,

*With love and the sincere hope
that you will be inspired
to seek out and explore Nature
as your Papa has.*

WARNING

Exploring the Grand Canyon can be very risky. Most visitors and hikers pay attention to safety warnings and dangerous conditions, but a small number tend to leave their common sense in the vehicle they arrived in. Please respect the potential dangers associated with hiking and exploring in the extreme wilderness, and remain acutely aware of your personal skills and limitations. Trail conditions and weather can change quickly and dramatically. Although trail descriptions and directions are accurate at the time of publication, unexpected trail and road closures are common events. The author and publisher of this book assume no responsibility or liability for the safety, judgment, or preparedness of our readers. Visitors intending to hike, camp or explore the Grand Canyon should contact the National Park Service for current weather, trail, camping and river conditions and possible restrictions:

Grand Canyon National Park

(928) 638-7875

https://grca_bic@nps.gov/

or

https://www.nps.gov/grca/planyourvisit/trail-closures.htm

TABLE OF CONTENTS

Dedication vii
WARNING viii
Acknowledgements x
Preface xiii
Introduction 13
1 First Steps 19
2 Adventures And Mis-Adventures At Thunder River . . 23
3 Grandview Trail And Horseshoe Mesa . . . 39
4 A Day Hike To Prove A Point To Myself . . . 51
5 Rim-To-Rim Logistics And Adventures . . . 57
6 The Powell Plateau: Find Your Own Bliss . . . 73
7 A Few Favorite East Rim Hikes 81
8 Clear Creek, Cheyava Falls,
     And Discovery Of Possible Human Remains. . . 95
9 Sumner Wash Revisited 103
10 Fun On The Colorado River 107
11 Helpful Tips And Lessons Learned . . . 123
Epilogue 131

ACKNOWLEDGEMENTS

No one writes a book by himself—especially a first time author. I have been fortunate to spend time in the Grand Canyon with countless friends over the last forty-five years. Many of them have been immeasurably helpful in remembering or verifying dates and trip details I had either forgotten or, in some cases, had tried to put out of my mind.

My profound thanks for guidance and project support go out to Hazel Clark and Tom Martin of Vishnu Temple Press. Good friends Tom Bennett, Ann Coury, Pruitt Layton, Jim McCarthy, Kathie Flannigan-Moore, Brian Smith, and Karen Smith helped with constructive feedback, fact checking, and, in some cases, their own memories of our many Canyon experiences together. Successful authors and friends Michael Ghiglieri, Tom Myers, and Marsha Ward willfully lent their proven guidance and support. Family members Brian Elston and Marilyn Elston believed in the value of collecting and publishing my lifetime of unique experiences, and provided much needed encouragement and proof reading. Without the editing, endorsement, critique, and encouragement of this entire group, I likely would have kept most of my Grand Canyon knowledge and learning experiences to myself.

Finally, the many long sojourns away from home, and occasional times I was overdue and didn't return on the day expected, were squarely shouldered by my wife, Rosemary—my first and most attractive hiking and exploring partner. She provided encouragement to follow my dreams, freedom and enough rope to tackle remote and seldom explored areas, and steadfast care and support of our family when I wasn't there. I was, however, there in spirit, as you were with me.

PREFACE

The wonders of the Grand Canyon cannot be adequately represented in symbols of speech, nor by speech itself. The resources of the graphic arts are taxed beyond their powers in attempting to portray its features. Language and illustration combined must fail.
     Major John Wesley Powell

    I stood at Mather Point, a typically crowded South Rim viewpoint and stared in awe. I seemed suddenly alone as others pushed past me for photos. My breath grew short in the cold afternoon wind, and the crowds and noise faded and disappeared. There, before my unbelieving eyes, lay the harsh, skeletal bones of the earth fully exposed. Mother Nature's beautiful and protective skin of forests, lakes, snows and soils was missing. Much like staring at a morbid traffic accident, my mind was transfixed and overwhelmed. Nothing else mattered as I struggled to process what I was seeing. I had more questions than answers. What massive forces could have caused this harsh and cataclysmic gash in the earth's crust? How many eons must this process have taken, and where did everything go that had once been here?

    As my numbed senses slowly returned, my fifteen-year-old mind was spinning but unable to come up with any answers–just more questions. As we departed the viewpoint and made our way toward more familiar sights such as food and gift shops, the questions and confusion in my mind continued. Does anyone understand how the Grand Canyon was formed? How far back into the earth's history can we see? And, is there any way to hike down into that canyon so I can witness Mother Nature's bones and inner beauty more closely?

    In retrospect, I was unknowingly beginning to develop a life plan for myself. I had to come back and begin exploring for answers. I needed to know and understand everything I could about this unique and tantalizing place only a few hours from my home. I would come back. I would study geology in college. I had to get to the bottom of this mysterious place. It turned out that the fledging plans I made that day served as a silent but prevailing wind for the rest of my life.

Today, after more than a year (400+ days) of hiking, rafting, and experiencing the Grand Canyon during the past 45 years, I am proud and humbled to realize that my plans were achieved. I have seen things most people have never seen. I have followed the trails and footsteps of ancient peoples who eked out a sparse, artistic, and meaningful existence on top and beneath the rims of the canyon. I have witnessed the delicate tapestry of life and death in one of the last extreme and remote places on earth. I have been fortunate to share many of my most favorite hiking and rafting destinations with close friends and family. And, at this point in my life, I feel a responsibility to be an advocate for this special place that has become my refuge, my church, and my home away from home.

The best way I know to represent my experiences, and also advocate on behalf of the Grand Canyon, is to write. This book offers up some of my most favorite hikes, a few of my worst and painfully naïve experiences, glimpses into some interesting history, tips and lessons learned, and a few recommendations for aspiring hikers, river runners, and explorers.

I sincerely hope you enjoy my first publication. Better yet, I hope you have the opportunity to visit the Grand Canyon. It is certainly this country's *grandest* national park. When President Theodore Roosevelt dedicated the Grand Canyon as a National Monument in 1908, he put his thoughts into more eloquent words than I could ever hope to:

> *Leave it as it is. You cannot improve on it. The ages have been at work on it, and man can only mar it. What you can do is keep it for your children, and for all who come after you, as the one great sight which every American should see.*

INTRODUCTION

Of all the paths you take in life, make sure a few of them are dirt.
John Muir

I was born in the Midwest, and am forever grateful that my parents moved our family to Arizona when I was six years old. I feel fortunate to have grown up in Arizona's Sonoran desert-the hottest in North America, where coyote and roadrunner sightings were our daily entertainment, and where nearly every plant was either thorny or poisonous, or both. With little annual rainfall, our major storms were more dust and sand than actual rain. We did our share of camping in the high country and exploring in the desert, and Boy Scouts introduced me to the wonders of hiking.

The Grand Canyon got under my skin at an early age. With more than a year spent in the Grand Canyon (400 hiking days spread over the past 45 years), approximately 4,500 miles hiked, and several Colorado River rafting trips in the log books, I am fortunate to have seen and experienced it in a way few others have. I often dreamed that I was one of the fortunate people who worked for the National Park Service (NPS) at Grand Canyon. However, just getting to-and-from the South Rim of the Grand Canyon is a 500-mile round-trip excursion from home for me. In my wandering mind, my ideal job was to work at Phantom Ranch or at the South or North Rim. My idyllic days off would be spent in hikes with my trusty backpack, an assortment of energy bars, a few quarts of electrolytes…and an occasional beer offered by a friendly river running group who would take pity on me. However, when I wrenched my mind back to reality, I knew I had a responsible and demanding job with a major aerospace corporation. While personal time off was a scarce commodity, my close-knit group of office friends more than offset the stress and demanding travel schedule. In fact, some of my friends proved to have the necessary stamina, curiosity and blind trust to take time off to accompany me on many of my treks.

One of the sincere pleasures of my hiking career has been organizing trips into the Canyon for friends and family members. If I find a very special place, I typically plan return trips with a few capable and curious friends. For example, I've now taken seven groups to Thunder River and Deer Creek. The first trip to my most favorite area happened to also be my first real backpacking trip, and I did spectacularly poorly! However, after my toenails grew back and the leg cramps and bloody blisters were long forgotten, I began to realize what a wonderful experience it had actually been. I decided to go back. I knew I could do better the next time.

Over the years, I've been fortunate to take my 75-year-old parents and one of my three siblings, my youngest sister and her family, on river and backpacking trips. Dozens of friends and co-workers have put their faith in me to visit many of my other favorite spots. It's rewarding to see how people grow closer when they've shared a special experience, and particularly when they have participated in planning the adventure. Nothing brings people closer than an all day, sunbaked hike topped off with a gritty wind storm or downpour while trying to cook and eat a dehydrated meal. Camaraderie continues to build as evening entertainment often includes trying to stand up without help or assisting friends treat blisters or rashes in places they never knew they had. A few days of standing knee deep in the ice cold Colorado River while trying to pee is enough to meld most people into a close-knit group with shared experiences and stories to tell their friends.

Exploring the depths of Grand Canyon is also about problem solving, which is one of the reasons I find it so appealing. How many people should be in my group? What if someone is seriously hurt, who will stay with the injured person while someone else hikes out to find help? There is also strength in numbers, but only up to a point. People can reduce backpack weight by sharing tents, water filters, stoves, cameras and emergency supplies. But, taking too many people tends to slow hiking progress since the group can only be as fast as the slowest hiker. Differing personalities can make or break a backpacking or river trip. Is everyone as excited as I am? Who will be the strongest and weakest hikers? Who will want to read a book or write in their journal when the rest of us are preparing dinner or cleaning up? Who enjoys a physical challenge? And, who will surprise me with their pure joy of being down *in* the Canyon rather than viewing it from the top? Finally, the stories you hear, and the things you learn about friends when they are relaxed and away from the daily grind, can be hilarious, illuminating, endearing and intimate. As they say, "*What happens in the depths of the Canyon is meant to forever stay below the rim.*"

Dropping below the rim on a hiking adventure means leaving 99% of the tourists on the rims behind. It means not knowing what to expect but necessarily being prepared for most anything. I have been sun baked, wind-burned, rained on, snowed on, snowed in, and too thirsty to talk. I have been "temporarily misplaced," totally lost, cliffed-out, worn out and once, but only once, ready to give up. I have found injured people, dehydrated people, incoherent people, dumb people and, sadly, several dead people. Circumstances leading to some, but not all of these events are discussed in this book.

This is not a "*How To*" book on hiking or rafting the Grand Canyon. There are plenty of excellent guide books, photography and poetry collections, geology primers and historical references written by those who have been immersed in the Grand Canyon more than I can even imagine. This book is a collection of personal stories about some of the most memorable places I've been privileged to experience. Each chapter includes some interesting information on history, geology, etc. Also, over my hiking and river running career I've learned what types of clothing, footwear and backpacking gear works best for me, and some chapters give brief reference to these items.

The most important thing I've learned, and it has come to guide my perspective on life, is that the Grand Canyon is a different experience for everyone. Simply put, *"You get what you give."* According to the National Park Service, most tourists visiting the iconic Grand Canyon today spend three hours there-including gift shops and restaurants. Yet, in 1920 the average tourist stayed three weeks. In a survey conducted by the Environmental Protection Agency they found that people in the United States spend 87 percent of their time indoors, mostly at either home or work. Certainly, a lot has changed in nearly 100 years. The speed of everyday life has increased, expectations have changed, people have changed, and it is convenient to vicariously experience others' Grand Canyon explorations via YouTube or Facebook. Everything has changed-except the Grand Canyon. It awaits you, your curiosity, your precious time, and your spirit of adventure. You will gain from it at least as much as you give.

So, what do I recommend you do and see? If you only have a few hours at the Grand Canyon, take a walk. Feel the early morning breeze as the cooler air on the rim almost imperceptibly slips into the warmer abyss below. Enjoy the variety of life as you watch unique Abert's and Kaibab squirrels shamelessly soliciting hand-outs. Mule deer and huge Rocky Mountain elk (introduced from Yellowstone National Park) are abundant in the forests and are often seen from the roadways within the park. If luck is with you, it's possible to discover an elusive Bighorn sheep standing still in hopes of not being noticed. Perhaps you will spot a rare California condor flying effortlessly on the updrafts overhead. Look for a white number under its 9'6" wing span. Today, each bird is closely monitored after the species dwindled to a scant 22 birds in the wild in 1987. As a result of near-extinction, the few remaining birds were captured and put into protective captivity. The Peregrine Fund and the San Diego and Los Angeles zoos have carefully managed a successful comeback of the species. Today, 71 known condors fly freely in Northern Arizona and Southern Utah, and the worldwide population of 439 continues to grow.[1] The expansive Grand Canyon and Vermilion Cliffs areas of Arizona and Southern Utah provide a suitable and sustainable environment for condors to thrive and reproduce as they once did. If you enjoy birds, you are in luck. There are more than 300 species recorded at the Grand Canyon. Don't forget the variety of people, too! With nearly 5 million visitors a year, there are more people from other countries than there are from the United States.

If you have more time at the Grand Canyon, visit the wonderful exhibits to learn something new about the geologic, human, and vast cultural history. Ask a park ranger how it's possible that two very long suspension bridges somehow made it to the bottom of the Grand Canyon to span one of the nation's wildest and largest rivers. Use the free shuttle service, or rent a bicycle at Bright Angel Bicycles, and pedal

The massive fireplace at Hermit's Rest. Courtesy of NPS.

the West Rim Bike Trail. Have your picture taken in front of the massive fireplace at Hermit's Rest. Enjoy the sunrise or sunset, or both. Take time to see the many historic photographs placed here-and-there throughout the hotels, restaurants and visitor centers. For a change of pace, visit the Grand Canyon Pioneer Cemetery near the Shrine of the Ages. There are very few cemeteries located in national parks and this one, established in 1922, is listed on the National Register of Historic Places. Many Grand Canyon pioneers, national park officials and Harvey Girls and their spouses, are buried in this beautiful setting. Be sure to look for the Airline Memorial that pays homage to victims of the 1956 mid-air collision over the Grand Canyon. This accident killed 128 people and was the genesis for creation of the Federal Aviation Administration.

Lucky you if your visit takes you to the much more remote and much less visited North Rim. The additional 1000' in elevation means slightly cooler weather, spruce, fir and aspen trees, and wonderful meandering meadows best seen during the drive on Highway 67 leading to the North Rim. Look for wildlife in the early mornings and late afternoons near the edges of the meadows. Wild turkey, deer, elk, and even buffalo are often seen. Last, but certainly not least, walk one of the many trails on the rim or down into the Canyon for a bit. You won't have to go too far to lose most of the crowds. As always, be prepared with adequate food and water and know your limitations. Don't end up like some of the unfortunate people you will read about in these pages.

My sincere hope is that in reading this book, you discover something new about one of Nature's greatest gifts to us. Whether experienced from the rims, the trails, or the river, the Grand Canyon offers something for everyone. As for me, I set out at an early age to discover the Grand Canyon and ended up discovering just as much about myself. As I dug into little known history, studied detailed topographic maps, and planned and made countless difficult but successful treks, I gained self-confidence, better attention to details, physical endurance, and a true appreciation of the natural world. Today, I have no doubt that the contour lines on my face are due to my studying, and then exploring, the contour lines on the many maps I reviewed in pursuit of new and remote places to explore and better understand in The Grand Canyon.

1. Public release of California Condors will be Held Saturday, Sept 27 at Vermilion Cliffs National Monument; July 30, 2014. The Peregrine Fund; http://www.peregrinefund.org/news-release/302.

Approaching the Kaibab Suspension Bridge Over the Colorado River. Courtesy of NPS.

CHAPTER ONE

First Steps

*I go to Nature to be soothed and healed,
and to have my senses put in order.*
John S. Burroughs

I remember thinking it couldn't get much better than this! It was early November, 1972, and I was at the Grand Canyon South Rim with my college sweetheart, Rosemary. We were taking an Introduction to Geology class at Scottsdale Community College and this was our first field trip. We had been dating for a year and were in several classes together. We eventually took every geology and mineralogy class the college offered.

Our assignment was to walk down the Bright Angel Trail to the 1.5 Mile Rest House and take notes of the geologic features we saw. What I remember clearly was that it was miserably cold and windy and the trail was somehow both icy and muddy at the same time. We hadn't walked more than 15 minutes down the trail when I noticed a fluorescent orange stocking cap in the snow bank to my right. Thinking it was just what I needed to keep my ears warm, I trudged uphill about 20 feet through knee-deep snow to the stocking cap and pulled. It took quite a bit of pulling to detach the cap from the snow. When it finally broke free, I nearly passed out. Under the stocking cap was a person's head! The hair was wet and the skin was patchy blue and white, and frozen. I didn't really know what to do, but impulse told me to hike up. I trudged uphill in the snow bank to the next trail switchback and headed to the first place I could find, the Kolb Studio on the Rim.[1] When I breathlessly told the woman at the cash register I needed to report a dead body, she very calmly picked up the phone, spoke to someone for less than 30 seconds, and told me in very certain words not to go anywhere. She was a professional…I was a mess!

It wasn't long before two National Park Service officials showed up with a stretcher with a bike wheel attached in the middle. An ominous looking black vinyl body bag lay strapped and waiting on top. I walked downhill with them back to where I had found the frozen body and they methodically took charge. Surprisingly, there was no questioning for me. It must have been clear from the tracks in the snow that this was not a crime scene. It was, however, a sad scene. It took the officials only a few minutes to photograph, package, and begin transporting the frozen body back up the trail. Our geology instructor advised us to call our parents in case there were any news reports of a death at the Grand Canyon.

Today, more than 42 years after this discovery, and as part of the process of writing this book, I finally learned who the person I discovered was. With generous assistance from friends, Michael Ghiglieri and Tom Myers, co-authors of *Over the Edge: Death Beneath the Rim*,[2] I learned who I had come face-to-face with on that cold, sad day. She was an 18-year-old teenager from Wisconsin named Robin Ruth Myers. Robin had a history of mental illness, and committed suicide by jumping off Maricopa Point on the South Rim of the Canyon. No one saw her fall to her death, which explained why no one had been looking for her. She lay frozen, a suicide note in her pocket, until a cold, teenaged geology student spotted an orange stocking cap and wanted it for himself. For the record, I never took the hat.

Despite this unfortunate incident, it was only a few months before I returned to the Grand Canyon. Family friends asked me to accompany them for an Easter weekend trip. When they picked me up at home on Saturday morning, I waved good-bye to my grandfather who was helping pick the relentless weeds at our desert home in Scottsdale. I told him I'd see him in a few days. Strangely, he replied "No, you won't." I assumed he was going on a trip that I didn't know about. After weeding all day in the warm April weather, he drove home to his apartment in Phoenix. He put dinner in the oven, sat down in his favorite chair, newspaper in his hands, and never woke up. Neighbors smelled his dinner burning and found him at peace. My arrival home the next day was, of course, a sad one. I was beginning to wonder whether I should ever return to the Canyon. Two visits and two deaths-not a good track record so far.

1. The Kolb Studio was built in 1904 by brothers Emery and Ellsworth Kolb. These two energetic photographers would take pictures of tourists riding mules 4.5 miles down the Bright Angel Trail to Indian Gardens. One or both of the brothers would then quickly hike back out of the Canyon to their studio, process the photos, and sell them to the dusty, trail-worn tourists at the end of the day. Today, the studio continues to cling to the very edge of the Grand Canyon and has undergone numerous additions and enhancements. It is listed on the National Register of Historic Places, and is a "*must see*" for South Rim visitors seeking books, history, artwork and a great view.

2. Readers interested in learning more about the vast array of deaths in the Grand Canyon, including the worst civilian air disaster of its day (1956), which led to formation of the Federal Aviation Administration (FAA), should read *Over the Edge: Death in Grand Canyon* by Michael P. Ghiglieri and Thomas M. Myers. Puma Press, Flagstaff, AZ.

Kolb Studio at the top of the Bright Angel Trail on a sunnier day

Dave and Rosemary, November, 1972 and January, 2016.

CHAPTER TWO

Adventures and Mis-Adventures at Thunder River

Been there, done that. Then, been there several more times because, apparently, I never learn.
author unknown

After graduating from Scottsdale Community College, I still had the "geology bug" but also thought I needed a back-up plan in case I couldn't successfully get through the physics and calculus classes required to actually earn a geology degree. I decided that Northern Arizona University (NAU) fit perfectly with my geologic plans, and was also pleased to learn that they taught business classes, too, in the event I needed to implement my ill-defined back-up plan. Rosemary had always wanted to be a teacher so she headed to Arizona State University (ASU) for her elementary education degree. It was the first time we were away from each other in more than two years.

I settled into my dorm room at NAU's new South Campus facilities and awaited the arrival of my roommate whom I hoped would be somewhat like me. After a day and night by myself, I answered the eventual knock on my door and came face-to-face with an apprehensive Brian Smith, a history major from San Diego, California. Brian had come to NAU with a good friend named Chip, and they intended to be roommates. However, a fateful mix-up occurred and Brian's first real test at his new university was to make friends with me.

It wasn't long before we realized we had a lot in common. We both had girlfriends back home and, in fact, their middle names were even the same. Brian had a strong interest in archaeology that dovetailed nicely with my passion for geology. As the semester progressed, he did very well in school. On the other hand, my geology studies were progressing at a more "tectonic" pace. I only received two thirds of the credits I intended for the semester. Punch card computer coding and geometry would have to wait for a more mature and motivated student. I had graduated Summa Cum Laude from community college so the process of dropping classes was something I wasn't familiar with. Instead of formally dropping any classes at NAU, I simply stopped attending. Lacking the formality of notifying my professors of my dropping two classes I was humbled, but not completely deterred, by the significant demise of my previous 4.0 GPA. I'm sure my parents thought I wasn't learning anything, but I had actually learned a lot.

My single semester experience in Flagstaff allowed me to hone my high altitude trout fishing skills, which were severely lacking due to my Sonoran Desert upbringing. Brian and I were also able to slip away to Needles, California a couple of times to learn slalom water skiing with our girlfriends. I also worked part-time at a local paint store, which provided me with spending money to occasionally hop into my truck and speed downhill to Phoenix to visit Rosemary who was thriving at ASU. On occasion, I even had some homework to do! Finally, there was always tennis or football to play with Brian and other friends who needed stress relief from their constant studies. As a good friend, I was always available to help them relax and unwind.

With the fall semester coming to an end, it was time to put my "big boy" pants on and focus on what was important then and what would be important for my future. Brian and I had both decided to return to our respective homes and girlfriends. However, the die of friendship had been cast between us. We both continued our studies and graduated in fine academic shape. I was the Best Man at his wedding and a year later he was my Best Man. He and his wife eventually had a daughter and we followed a year or so later with the birth of our own beautiful daughter. A few years later we found out our wives were both pregnant again, this time with boys. What a surprise-our son was named Brian.

During the time between leaving NAU and eventually graduating with a business degree, Brian's fine dad, Smitty, had what he thought was a really great idea. He had read about a unique place named Thunder River in the Grand Canyon and decided he and his

[4] *Trout from Tapeats Creek.*

two sons should experience it in person. Brian invited me to join their trip, and I quickly agreed.

    Thunder River is a very unique place, indeed. It is one of the shortest and steepest rivers in North America, and is said to be one of the few rivers in the world that flows into a creek. In a vast, sunbaked desert landscape where water means life, and life is scarce, it gushes out of a narrow slit in the Redwall limestone at an average rate of 65 cubic feet-per-second. The cool water tumbles steeply past huge cottonwood trees and over mossy boulders as gravity escorts it a half-mile to its confluence with the much calmer, trout-laden Tapeats Creek. It was said to be Barry Goldwater's favorite place in the Grand Canyon. Barry was one of the first 100 people to raft through the Grand Canyon when he joined a Norm Nevills trip in 1940. He made the two-mile trek from the Colorado River up Tapeats Creek to witness Thunder River for himself. After his river trip, he entertained crowds throughout Arizona with a slide show of Grand Canyon photographs. He came to realize he had a knack for public speaking, which may have been the impetus that spawned his long and successful political career.

Smitty was a self-made man with a great sense of adventure. I had previously enjoyed a successful, wind-blown San Juan River trip with Brian, Smitty, and a group of Boy Scouts, and the trip had been a great success. I was now looking forward to another one of his great adventures. Smitty's idea was that this trip would only be the first of many to Thunder River. He intended our group to bring, and then cache, items such as cast iron cooking pans, large amounts of Bisquick, kerosene lanterns and fuel, etc. His end goal was that we would eventually be able to hike in with just food and supplies and, therefore, stay longer. Someday in the future, when we had decided there was no more to see or discover at Thunder River, he planned to make a river trip, stop for a day at the mouth of Tapeats Creek, and hike upstream to retrieve all the heavy cooking and camping equipment we had labored over the years to cache.

I was anxious to participate and eager to try out my new Jansport "Rainier" model backpack. In those days, external packs (the metal frame is exposed) were much more prevalent than internal packs (the frame is often composite or metal and not visible) and mine was the top-of-the-line in its day. I had been doing some weekend backpacking trips in the Superstition Mountains east of Phoenix with my Coleman, plastic-framed backpack, so my new Jansport felt like a comfortable feather pillow. A very large feather pillow designed to hold lots of food and equipment.

I flew to Las Vegas with my new backpack as my checked luggage. I had never been to Vegas before and didn't know for sure what to expect. After landing, I headed toward Baggage Claim but made a brief stop to use the restroom. When I entered, I noticed a very well-dressed man loitering at the sink counter, and he seemed to be in no hurry to leave. I glanced over my shoulder a couple of times to note him idly watching me. I thought I was going to be robbed! When I approached the sinks to wash my hands, he cordially offered me a hand towel and my choice of colognes and a breath mint. A restroom attendant in an airport! This was all new to me, and I'm sure I still owe him a tip. In hindsight, I was probably a bit of a curiosity to him in that I was wearing new zip-off cargo pants, new hiking boots, and a large brimmed hiking hat...not typical resort wear for Vegas.

After spending the night in Vegas, we headed to the North Rim Lodge. The long drive through the sparse desert eventually led us up the Kaibab Plateau where we arrived in the pine trees overlooking the Grand Canyon. The night before our big adventure, we spread out everything we had brought along for our hike on the hotel beds. Holy crap...what a lot of stuff! There were a couple of kerosene lanterns and a gallon or two of fuel, heavy metal frying pans and pots with lids, ropes and tents, a Dutch oven, the ever-present coffee pot, a couple of very large boxes of Bisquick, a few round loaves of bread the size of Olympic curling stones, a six pack of beer, a five gallon plastic bucket and lid for each of us, and lots of food for breakfast and lunches. I noted there seemed to be no food for dinners other than items like dehydrated veggies and mashed potatoes, so I asked what was planned for our three nights of dinners. The disturbing answer was, *"We are going to catch fish."* Fortunately, Brian and I both brought fishing poles and had fishing licenses (a must in a National Park). We let Smitty divide the cargo between us, but Brian and I sensed that most of the really heavy stuff ended up in our piles. Once everything was in our packs, Brian and I had to help each other pick up and put on our packs. They were so heavy I worried about bending the new aluminum frame. Oh well, I thought, how hard can it be-it's all downhill.

We began our hike at Monument Point and had our hiking sticks, except for Brian who brought a 6-iron golf club as his support staff. The start of the hike plays a cruel trick on hikers. The first half-mile is uphill and over Millet Knoll (elevation 7206') before finally beginning the long, 12-mile descent to the Tapeats Creek campsite at about 2,000 feet. We would be hiking down a vertical mile. Even today, I smile each time I begin this hike when I see the heavy clothing hikers often shed and leave hanging on branches or under bushes on this sweaty first section of the trail.

Thunder River can be accessed by two separate and unique trails, as well as one very remote and seldom used trail. I typically hike the Bill Hall Trail because it's a few miles shorter than the other trail that begins at Indian Hollow. The disadvantage to the Bill Hall Trail is that it begins at 7100' vs. 6400' at Indian Hollow. For hikers with interest in hieroglyphics, the Indian Hollow Trail has some great rock art whereas there is very little I've ever seen on the Bill Hall Trail. In addition to these two trails, there is a third, very remote and seldom used trail that is more a route than a distinct trail.

I had heard rumors of a difficult, but do-able route to Tapeats Cave, but until I began writing this book, I had little information and no confirmed trip reports about it. The Big Saddle Cowboy Trail, first established in the late 1800s for geologic exploration, eventually became a stock trail to herd cattle off the North Rim into the warmer climates of the Esplanade and Crazy Jug Canyon areas. There are several difficult trail sections in the Toroweap and Coconino formations that require very sure-footing, bouldering, and rappelling skills, but there are also established by-passes for these otherwise difficult areas. You will likely not encounter anyone else in this remote and largely unknown region. In fact, it's so remote that in 1985 it took search and rescue personnel more than two weeks to locate a missing aircraft that had disappeared during a flight to Utah. Today, the wreckage of the yellow Piper Cub is encountered during the descent toward the Esplanade. The National Park Service is a necessary and essential source of up-to-date information on water, accessibility, and difficulty if you decide to do a loop hike incorporating this route as your entry point.

The Bill Hall and Indian Hollow trails meet on my most favorite geologic layer in the Grand Canyon, the Esplanade. This layer is ochre-red, and the many rock depressions become water pockets, or tinajas, after a good rain. If the water remains long enough, invertebrates such as midges and fairy shrimp hatch and bring these small, ephemeral pools to life. In the setting sun, the water pockets shine like an ocean of diamonds.

The many shallow caves and overhangs near the junction of the two trails are a good place to cache an extra gallon of water per person for your return hike out. I always put my name and a permanent marker note such as, "You can have this water after (pick a date)." With this information, if you end up not needing your own water, someone else who might really need it can feel free to take it. Unfortunately, this is also a typical place to find other hiker's empty and discarded containers. Clip a couple to your backpack on your hike out. It just might make you feel a bit better, too, during the long, grinding set of 50-some switchbacks up through the Coconino Sandstone to your vehicle at the top.

Our band of four intrepid hikers made steady progress all morning. I occasionally snacked on trail mix, but didn't drink much water because I didn't know how long my four quarts needed to last me. Today, and in hindsight, I realize that my stomach is my best canteen. If I'm going to store water, I begin by filling my "internal canteen" with a quart or so of electrolyte-enhanced water while still at the trailhead. I'm going to carry it anyway, so I might as well carry some inside of me.

By noon, we were making our way west across the beautiful Esplanade with its display of caves, hoodoos and cool places begging to be explored during a more leisurely opportunity. We came to the edge and got our first glimpse of the Colorado River still quite aways below us. We descended 1000' or so through the next layer of rock, the Redwall. This area of the trail is exposed to full afternoon sun, as is the next geologic feature, Surprise Valley, at the base of the Redwall. Once in Surprise Valley, we came to a "T" trail intersection. The trail to the left takes hikers to Thunder Spring, a true oasis in the desert. The spring cascades its way down to Tapeats Creek where we had a permit to camp for a few nights.

The trail to the right takes hikers to Upper Deer Creek Falls, Deer Creek Narrows and Lower Deer Creek Falls. The creek becomes a 100' waterfall into a plunge pool next to the Colorado River. There are no other trail options, but that didn't stop an NAU student hiking alone, and without a permit, from getting fatally lost.

In mid-July 2009, Bryce Gillies, age 20, set out to celebrate his 20th birthday. He had read an article in Backpacker Magazine describing Thunder River as *"The toughest long weekend hike in Grand Canyon."* He cryptically told friends at NAU that he was hiking to a secret waterfall in the Grand Canyon that no one knew about. He intended to go with another hiker, but she wasn't able to go with him. Bryce was an Eagle Scout and an engineering student with hiking experience. He had a GPS with him and also hand-written trail notes from the magazine's website. He crossed the Esplanade but eventually ran out of water. After descending through the Redwall, he reached the "T" intersection in Surprise Valley where he took a major wrong turn. Based on footprints he left in the sand, later discovered by Search and Rescue personnel, he mistakenly descended the Bonita Creek drainage. His thirst drove him onward toward the water he knew was close. He continued making his way downward over the perilous ledges until he could go no further. Eventually, he was out of options. He could not ascend or descend. He had no rope and the next ledge was 100' below him.

After Bryce was reported missing, a massive search was launched with personnel from Bryce, Zion and Grand Canyon national parks. On the fourth day of the search, a helicopter pilot spotted a white plastic shopping bag. It contained canned food that had been drained of its liquids. From there, footprints led into the Bonita Creek drainage. Two Search and Rescue personnel rappelled down the various difficult ledges until darkness fell.

They bivouacked on a ledge for the night and discovered Bryce Gillies' badly sunburned body the next day. The temperature was 106° in the shade. Bonita Creek is the next drainage downstream of Thunder River. Bryce may have been able to occasionally hear the sound of the Thunder Springs waterfall he so desperately sought but couldn't reach as he made his fateful descent. His vehicle was found at the trailhead. It contained nearly a gallon of water. In one of a few final messages on his cell phone he wrote, *"Life is good whether it is long or short."* Bryce was one of 12 people who died in the Grand Canyon in 2009.[1]

Upon arriving at the T-trail intersection, we took the left trail toward Thunder Spring. It was a hot day and, in hindsight, I hadn't eaten enough food or drunk nearly enough water, although I had plenty in my heavy backpack. The trek through Surprise Valley is a series of undulating ups and downs but nothing too steep. What we couldn't appreciate about the landform of Surprise Valley is that it became a giant convection oven even in the early fall months. Sunlight reflects off every side of the steep valley walls and intensifies the already hot afternoon temperatures.

As we made our way across Surprise Valley, the environment seemed to get eerily still. The only sounds were our footsteps crunching along the sandy and dusty trail. Gradually, and barely noticeably, I started to feel weak and light-headed. My tongue was swollen and I had stopped sweating. The last thing I remember was watching the sun go down very quickly as I fell backward onto my new backpack and passed out. I'm not sure how long I was unconscious, but I later learned that Brian, Peter and Smitty dragged my overheated body to some shade under a large bush. We all stayed in the scant shade awhile, drank water, and cooled off just a bit as we regained some sense of where we were. Realistically, we were all suffering under the heat of the mid-day sun.

When we restarted our trek out of Surprise Valley, we had to cross one more ridge to make the entrance into Tapeats Creek Canyon. We were all wary of my weak condition and our brush with the uncertainties of the Grand Canyon. I recall basically just mumbling incoherently in some type of strange conversation with my hiking companions.

As we finally crested the ridge and transitioned from the heat of Surprise Valley, we surveyed the world of lush greenery that framed Thunder Springs and the cascades of Thunder River below us. We could barely keep from running down the trail. The half-mile trail to our much needed oasis seemed to take an eternity to cross.

Once we reached the fast flowing, pure waters of Thunder Spring, we quickly jettisoned our packs, took off our heavy and dusty boots, and waded into the cool water to drink and try to revive ourselves. Subsequent training as part of my Wilderness First Responder (WFR) certification taught me that I had experienced severe heat stroke, or hyperthermia. I was unable to sweat or focus my thoughts, and all I wanted to do was drink. And drink I did. I vaguely recall sitting at the edge of the misty waterfall chugging a few quarts of water over the course of an hour or more. I'm sure my hiking companions were worried about me, but they didn't over-react or seem unusually concerned. In retrospect, the key to dealing with heat stroke is to drink before you are thirsty, and to understand that by the time you are incoherent, the damage has already been done.

As strange as it may seem, it's also possible to suffer from drinking too much water, especially during serious exercise such as hiking. A potentially life-threatening condition, hyponatremia, can be caused by drinking so much water that electrolyte balances become diluted and abnormal. Sodium, a critically important electrolyte, can become so diluted that cells in the body swell and cause a decline in total blood volume. Exercise-Associated Hyponatremia (EAH) is rare, but cases have been increasing as rim-to-rim running and similar extreme sports are gaining in popularity. In 2015, a female Grand Canyon hiker died after completing a 5 hour hike. Her sodium levels indicated excessive quantities of water had been consumed. In recent studies, football players, military personnel, marathon runners, police officers, canoe paddlers, cyclists, and triathletes have all shown elevated levels of EAH. Incidences of alarming levels of EAH have been noted as high as 18% in Ironman triathlons, 28% in marathons, 50% in endurance cycling, and 51% in 100-mile ultramarathons. The lesson here is to drink before you're thirsty, drink when you are thirsty, eat salty snacks, pay attention to your body, and never drink excessively.[2]

After resting and rebuilding our strength, we continued the remaining 1.5 miles downhill hike to the campsites at the confluence of Tapeats Creek and Thunder River. Even that short hike was not without danger, as Brian walked within a foot of a coiled rattlesnake under a tree root. I spotted the snake only after he had walked right next to it.

In the early 1980s there were only three campsites. We chose the first one on the right that had a great 12' boulder at the back of the site. After setting up camp and our mega tent, with very little assistance from me, some of the guys fished and actually caught a few nice trout for dinner. They had trout and re-hydrated mixed vegetables and made a small dent in the loaves of Sheepherder bread. I trust it was a good meal but am not sure. I had water with a side of water for dinner.

After a good night's sleep, our plan was to leave the campsite and hike downstream with daypacks to the Colorado River. It's a beautiful and relatively easy two-mile hike following and crossing Tapeats Creek several times. This is where at least one hiking pole is beneficial as a "third leg" when crossing swift water. The elevation loss from our campsite to the Colorado River was only a few hundred feet, and both sides of the creek were overgrown with lush vegetation. I have read that a trained eye can spot Anasazi Indian ruins in the cliffs above the creek. One of the granaries or storage areas, named the Mystic Eye, has eluded me on each trip. Apparently, I don't have trained eyes, because during seven watchful trips to this area I have never seen them.

We departed camp with lunches, drinks, fishing poles and high expectations. I was about to fulfill my life-long dream of hiking all the way to the Colorado River. During our hike, a private helicopter flew close overhead and hovered for a while over Tapeats Spring before heading toward the river. Once we had arrived at the Colorado River, we were met by a river rafting group that was filming a documentary about the Grand Canyon. That explained the helicopter sighting. I recall they said something about making a movie about Major John Wesley Powell's grueling 1869 boat trip through the Grand Canyon. They were looking for extras for the film. The only one of us they showed interest in was Brian, who had a beard and apparently looked haggard enough to pass for one of the unfortunate members of the Major's crew.

We tried our luck fishing where the mouth of Tapeats Creek meets the Colorado River and had a lot of success. Once again we had caught fish for dinner, and this time I was feeling well enough to eat. Our fishing success was the envy of the other hikers we passed on our way back to the campsite. I have brought a small, collapsible fishing pole on all my return trips to Tapeats Creek and have always caught fish. On one trip I forgot to bring flies or spinners. Surprisingly, I caught two fish by just using a bare hook.

The return hike upstream to our campsite was uneventful, and our fish dinner was great. It was the first time I'd seen trout with pink flesh. That evening, during a card game by kerosene lantern, we were joined by a playful ringtail, often mistakenly called a ring-tailed cat, miner's cat or civet. Ringtails are actually members of the raccoon family, not the cat family, and are the "official" mammal of Arizona. It was the first one I'd ever seen, and it returned the next night as well to help keep our camp clean of any food scraps.

Our agenda for Day 3 was a hike up Tapeats Creek to see if we could find the headwaters. Tapeats Creek, named for the geologic layer from which it emerges, is the largest creek that originates in the Grand Canyon. There wasn't a trail in those days so we basically bushwhacked and slogged upstream. It was a glorious fall day-just hot enough that being wet from the waist down felt really good. We never actually reached the headwaters, but thanks to a northerly bend in the creek, we were able to see the slot cave that Tapeats flows out of in the distance. This area seemed to be begging for further exploration but I've never returned. Perhaps now that I'm retired and still in good health, I will add it to my Bucket List. I might even hike down the Big Saddle cowboy trail for a change of scenery.

On our final day at Tapeats, we departed camp in the afternoon for our designated campsite in Surprise Valley. Before we left, Brian and I found a place to cache the cooking gear, kerosene lamps, and extra gear and provisions for our planned return trips. On several subsequent trips, I have looked and looked but have never found our cache. Today, my experience and conscience wouldn't let me cache equipment without first checking the regulations and obtaining advance approval, if even possible, from the Park Service.

After a 45-minute uphill climb, we reached Thunder Spring and filled up everything that would hold water. The weather had begun changing rapidly, the winds picked up red, gritty dust, and by sunset we knew we were in for a pretty good late-season rainstorm. We never reached Surprise Valley and were forced to hole up for the night in a shallow overhang just north and above the trail at the edge of the plateau. We could occasionally hear Thunder Springs a few hundred feet below us, but the winds of the brewing storm soon masked the roar below with a greater roar from above. We weren't able to fix dinner that night, but we certainly enjoyed a full serving of Mother Nature's forces. We rested fitfully, sitting on the dusty cave floor and leaning against our backpacks, while the storm raged. The blackness of the canyon was occasionally lit up like an evening football game by brief but intense lightning flashes. We could hear rocks and boulders being dislodged and carried downstream in temporary streams. It was the first time I had witnessed the effects of static electricity as the hair on my arms and legs stood straight up. The acrid smell of ozone permeated the air, and the lightning flashes were immediately followed by thunder that seemed to be just feet away from us. A cave or overhang is one of the safest places to be during a lightning storm. The insects must have known this too, as we spent most of the night keeping spiders and scorpions off of ourselves.

At first light, we donned our packs and headed across Surprise Valley on the muddy trail. The hike up the Redwall on our way to the Esplanade was cooler, cloud-covered, and enjoyable. We hiked across the Esplanade to where we had cached our water and, once again, sought shelter as the rain returned. There's nothing quite as peaceful or as fragrant as a cool, morning rain in the desert. The smell of wet sagebrush added to the beauty of this special place. I remember the gentle rain, the red mud on my boots, and the camaraderie as if it happened just yesterday.

The remainder of the hike up to the trailhead was straightforward and filled with one unending switchback after another. Frequent breaks to take in the view toward the west are both necessary and highly recommended. In addition to catching your breath and grabbing a drink and snack, you will experience a truly unique view. Rather than a typical north-to-south view, you will experience a panoramic, east-to-west view of at least 50-75 miles. The Kaibab Plateau (North Rim) will be on your right, the Coconino Plateau (South Rim) on your left, and the magnificent Esplanade on full display in front of you. To the right, you may see faint sections of the trail from the Esplanade to the Indian Hollow trailhead and the large cliff and overhang where the haunting Ghost Rock petroglyphs can be found.

In the distance, and at the top edge of the South Rim, you can see Mt. Sinyala and Hualapai Hilltop. The hilltop is the staging area where up to 250 anxious hikers each day depart toward the isolated village of Supai 7.8 miles below, and the wondrous, travertine-blue waterfalls of Havasu Canyon an additional two miles further. The extremely remote village was the last place in the lower 48 states to receive permanent electricity and by today's standards seems to be many decades behind our fast-paced times. There's a saying on the Colorado Plateau about those of us who always seem to be in a rush: *"Don't worry, be Hopi!"* Havasu Canyon is a relaxing and beautiful inner-canyon destination that attracts hikers from around the world. All in all, this is perhaps one of my favorite viewpoints in the Grand Canyon, and one not usually enjoyed by the crowds.

By late afternoon, we had completed our hike back to Monument Point and were making the long drive toward paved roads, comfortable beds, and real ice cream shakes at the Jacob Lake Inn. Brian's wife, Kathy, had baked chocolate chip cookies that had been left in the van for our return drive. I recall the four of us finished about three dozen cookies by the time we were back on a firm, paved road.

My first real backpacking trip had been a mixture of failure and success. Although I was fortunate to have survived hyperthermia, I had some lingering souvenirs of the trip to deal with. I eventually lost seven toenails, and a couple of others remained black for several months but never came off, although I wish they would have. My hiking buddies had similar toe issues but, all-in-all, we agreed this had been one heck of a great trip.

Despite my abused toes, the most lasting effect of my first true backpacking trip was that I had been bitten big time by the Canyon Bug. I started making frequent backpacking trips, purchasing more and better equipment, attending guest lectures at REI, and making lists of places I intended to explore. Thankfully, Rosemary enjoyed backpacking too, and as our children grew we introduced them to hiking and eventually to backpacking. Surprisingly, it wasn't long before I had the urge to visit Thunder River again. This time it would be with a group of guys I worked with who all had some previous Grand Canyon experience. Despite tempting fate once again, I agreed to guide them to Thunder River and Deer Creek. I have now made seven treks to Thunder River and the nearby Deer Creek area, and am hoping for one more final trip with my two grandsons in a few years.

1. Information on the death of Bryce Gillies obtained from *Arizona Daily Sun*, Flagstaff, AZ; Staff Writer, Cyndy Cole. January 18, 2010.

2. *Exercise-associated Hyponatremia-Let's Stop Adding Insult to Injury with Our Treatment*; Martin D. Hoffman, MD, FACSM, FAWM; naemsp.org.

CHAPTER THREE

Grandview Trail and Horseshoe Mesa

There is no shame in making mistakes. The shame is in not admitting when you've made a mistake and not learning from it.
author unknown

The Boy Scout hike down the Grandview Trail to Horseshoe Mesa was intended to be the easier of the two hikes the troop leaders had arranged. Our troop was a large one and, with Presidents Day affording us a three-day weekend, the leaders had selected both an easy and a moderate Grand Canyon hike. The more experienced boys were to hike to the small village of Supai at the west end of the Grand Canyon and camp above Mooney Falls. My son, Brian, was not quite 12 years old and a new member of the troop. His age and entry-level status meant he was only eligible for the easy Grandview to Horseshoe Mesa hike. Had any of the leaders asked, they would have learned that Brian had already spent considerable time beneath the Canyon rim on several overnight backpacking trips with me.

The Grandview Trail was a great choice for an introductory hike. It's a three-mile descent to the campsites, and the trail is full of historical significance and beautiful views. It's also one of the steepest trails in the Grand Canyon as it drops 1,200' in the first ¾ of a mile. Hopi Indians collected minerals such as Malachite and Azurite on Horseshoe Mesa. In the late 1800s a prospector named Pete Berry improved the Hopi route down the canyon walls into a trail to support his two copper mines, the Grandview and Last Chance mines. He named his trail the Berry Trail. By 1907 the copper had played out but Berry gained notoriety by presenting samples of his copper ore at the 1906 World's Fair in Chicago. His ore was judged the most pure copper (70%) ever discovered in the world. However, the difficulties and costs associated with transporting the ore by mule train up 2700 vertical feet to the canyon rim, and then on to a smelter, proved too costly, and his two mines were eventually abandoned. Today, entrances to the mines have been covered with bat-friendly steel gates.

Brian was well prepared for Boy Scouts. In addition to lots of family hikes and camping trips, he had spent a few years in Cub Scouts and I had been his Den Leader. When I grew up in the wind-swept desert of what today is North Scottsdale, my Mom had been my Cub Scout Den Mother. To complete the leadership team, my Dad had been the Scoutmaster of the Cub Scout pack. With my load of heavy business travel, I knew I didn't have enough spare time to follow in his footsteps. However, the Den Leader position seemed right for me. It basically meant having weekly evening meetings at our house where we would work on crafts or projects, eat some sugary snacks, and generally get the boys hyped-up just in time for them to go home and try to fall asleep. On a few occasions, I couldn't get home from travel in time so my wife stepped in and successfully steered the 6-8 boys far better than I ever did. She was an elementary school teacher, and I assumed that a small group of boys would be easy compared to her typical classroom of 30+ kids. After all, how hard could it be to teach boys how to use pocket knives and carve my large collection of hotel soaps into arrowheads.

Our hike down the Grandview Trail to Horseshoe Mesa started out in typical fashion with much anticipation by everyone for a fun, three-day trip away from home. We had 7 or 8 boys and 4 adults who, like me, had day jobs and were looking forward to some quality time with their sons. Leaders of the troop had dutifully checked the weather forecast and reported that all was good for the next few days, and that a storm was due to arrive on Tuesday–the day after we hiked out. The hike is three miles of downhill with a vertical drop of 2,700' to a beautiful horseshoe-shaped plateau. Our plans were to eat lunch on the trail, set up tents in the early afternoon and then hike a mile or so, and down a few hundred feet, to a nearby water source where we would pump and purify water for our two night stay.

Our anxious group of boys and men cheerfully made good time as we descended toward the mesa. We sang scouting songs and talked about what we would see and do for the next couple of days. I had taken the rear position so that I could keep the herd moving and encourage any stragglers. By late morning, I noticed an increase in high, wind-swept clouds blowing in from the west at a worrisome rate. Lunch on the trail was accompanied by light rain, but the boys barely noticed in their excitement and their new boots. As Scouts, we had been taught to "Be Prepared" and a light rain wouldn't put a damper on our long-anticipated adventure!

We arrived at Horseshoe Mesa by 2:30 PM and established our camp for the next two nights. The troop owned several four person dome tents, and I had brought my low profile Marmot tent for myself and Brian. The winds had picked up considerably, and some of the men decided to erect a windscreen from an extra tarp so that the stoves wouldn't blow out when boiling water for dinner. A few of us gathered every vessel that would hold water and made the downhill hike to the spring to obtain our two day water supply. By the time we returned to camp, nightfall was approaching and the wind had kicked up a dust storm on the mesa. We made a unanimous decision to put the boys in their tents since the temperature had also dropped significantly. The adults put on their warmest gear and boiled water behind the makeshift wind screen for our dehydrated dinners. Everyone ate dinner in their tents while the winds continued to pick up speed. We eventually decided that everyone needed to remain in their tents, put on their warmest clothes, and get into their sleeping bags to ride out the storm. It was one of the longest and windiest nights of my life. I was glad to have Brian with me to witness what I'd only seen a couple of times before in my outdoor adventures.

Horseshoe Mesa is a Grand Canyon anomaly. At an elevation of 5240' it is less than half-way to the bottom of the Grand Canyon. It sticks out like a hitchhiker's thumb into the prevailing winds that flow end-to-end through the Canyon, which is 10-12 miles wide and 277 miles long. It is rich in mineral resources and, once discovered, has withstood more than its share of human activity and exploitation in the past hundred years or so.

As Brian and I rested in our tent, it occurred to me that it was an opportune time to complete an action item my wife had recently asked of me…to have the Birds and Bees discussion with him. I doubted he would leave the comfortable confines of our tent and hoped he would learn something new from our fatherly discussion. However, the conversation took about 30 seconds, during which I was convinced he needed no further input from The Old Man.

As the night progressed, the winds increased to a rage I'd never experienced before. People interviewed after tornadoes often say the winds sounded like a freight train and I can heartily confirm their description. Although the winds were often steady at perhaps 20-25 MPH, every few minutes Brian and I would hear the "freight train" noise winding its way through the canyon toward our tent. We quickly learned that we had only a few seconds to grab the internal tent poles and hold them as steady as possible while the freight train-like winds blew over us.

In the early morning hours, and without any noticeable sleep, I heard someone calling me. "Mr. Elston, Mr. Elston," a desperate voice was hollering through the relentless winds. I needed to investigate and, after bundling up and lighting my headlamp, I peered through the tent flaps. In the distance I could see the dome tents-all of which had collapsed during the night into sad, snow-dusted heaps. I heard my name once again and headed to the tent closest to mine. As I looked inside, one of the boys, Jarett, was out of his sleeping bag and sitting up. The others in the tent were awake, too, and their worried faces looked to me for reassurance. The collapse of their tent had allowed blown snow to sneak inside. It eventually melted and sought out the lowest spot in the tent…under Jarett's now wet sleeping bag. Like his sleeping bag, his clothes were wet, too. I found his backpack and took a look inside with hopes of finding dry clothes. What I found was something I recall to this day. In the beam of my headlamp I found a gallon Ziploc bag with a dry flannel shirt inside. In another Ziploc bag were dry pants. Remarkably, the pants bag also held a card Jarett's parents had packed for him that they knew he'd discover during the hike. It was a simple card saying how much they both loved him and that they were hoping he would have a fun and safe trip. I stayed with the boys for a half hour or so while Jarett warmed up and moved to a higher spot in the collapsed and damaged tent. I had been in a wicked snowstorm once before while overnighting at Camp Muir on Mt. Rainier. The group I was with then were all experienced climbers and backpackers being led by Rainier Mountaineering. Tonight's drama was a different story. I spent the rest of the night worrying about how much snow we could get, how long the storm might last, the minimal cold weather experience and equipment of our desert-based boys and leaders, and whether it was wise to stay two more days until our scheduled hike out on Monday.

I must have eventually fallen asleep because I awoke to quiet talking outside my tent. The other adult leaders were already up and milling around camp in a blinding snowstorm. Despite a night of wet snowfall, there was only 3-4" on the ground. Looking up toward the South Rim where our cars were parked was impossible because the entire rim was blanketed in ominous snow clouds. I joined the leaders in discussing what to do today since the weather would impact our planned map and compass workshop in the morning and our afternoon visit to the Cave of the Domes. After listening to their tentative plans, I spoke up and told them we needed to break camp and hike out as quickly as possible. My opinion was based on more than a hundred nights already spent in varying conditions in the Canyon, and I strongly felt the storm was likely to last through the day. A lengthy snowstorm would make the hike out extremely difficult, if not impossible, for some of our boys. I recommended we forego breakfast, grab our snack foods and leave immediately to hike out. Lacking firm plans from anyone else, and a bit surprisingly to me, the leaders agreed we needed to get moving as quickly as possible. We roused the boys, packed up our wet and sad tents, and left the excess water we had pumped the day before for future hikers. To my surprise, the boys were excited about hiking out a day earlier than planned. I know the adults were relieved, as well. We had all experienced a very long night and were not looking forward to a repeat performance.

Our group was in good spirits as we left camp. I pointed out some mine shafts and prospecting remnants from the late 1800s. The boys were happy because we were letting them eat near-frozen candy bars and trail mix in lieu of the more wholesome breakfast we had planned for them and were now carrying back up the trail. There was no time to boil water for a formal breakfast. We were in a race against time and the shortened winter days.

Not more than 15 minutes into our ascent, I spotted a man off to our right who was standing on a hill next to a large umbrella tent. When he saw me, he came running through the blowing snow while wildly waving his arms. I vividly recall the tan, canvas bib overalls he was wearing and how much he reminded me of Goober on the Andy Griffith show! With anxious breaths he asked, *"Where is the nearest phone?"* I replied that there was an emergency phone at the Tipoff, west of us a full day's hike away. He was visibly shaking when he explained, *"Me and my old man and my son hiked down late yesterday. My old man has a broken ankle and can't walk."* I had one of our adults take the lead with our group while I visited the wind-blown tent on the hill. It was quite a sight! Outside the tent was a large, two burner Coleman stove and a few empty soup cans. I couldn't believe someone had actually carried what had to be a 20-pound stove...and fuel! Inside was The old man, who, as "Goober" had accurately guessed, did indeed appear to have, at minimum, a severely sprained ankle. It was swollen to at least twice the size of his other ankle and was a colorful black, blue and yellow–much like a plump, aging banana. There was nothing I could do right then to evacuate their party. I loosely wrapped the colorful ankle with a compression wrap, told them to occasionally apply snow stuffed into a sock, and left them some pain reliever. Most importantly, I pointed out a shallow, abandoned mine shaft about 5 minutes downhill. I recommended they relocate everything from their wind-swept camp into the mine shaft in order to get out of the increasing snow and wind. I also told them where our troop's extra water was stashed and left them the uncooked breakfast and dinner food I had in my backpack. As I departed, I assured them I would send help, and strongly cautioned them not to leave the mine shaft area until they were rescued.

It didn't take long to find my group again because I could follow their tracks in the deepening snow. They were making a slow but steady pace, and a few of the boys were complaining about not having gloves. We stopped briefly while everyone either found their gloves or put socks and plastic bags over their hands. Some of the boys hiked with their hands under their armpits to make good use of their body heat.

We climbed steadily, but after a couple of hours we still couldn't see the rim. We had ascended into about 18" of snow and the trail was getting harder and harder to follow. Since no one had hiked the trail before us, the virgin snow covered the trail completely. In many places the bushes and trees were laden with the heavy, wet snow. They were bent over so much that they often blocked the trail. As the front man, I continually hit the branches with my hiking sticks to release the snow burden so that we could get under or through the trees.

It was around mid-day and I was becoming increasingly worried about us getting to our vehicles before darkness fell. Although I rarely choose to split up a group, the leaders and I made the tough decision to split into two smaller groups. I took four of the faster boys with me and the other leaders took the remaining boys. My group was in the lead, and I was "post-holing" the trail, which, in theory, would make it easier for the group behind us to hike in the snow that had already been trampled down. By following in our footsteps, they would also not wander off the trail we were plowing for them.

By the time we were within a few hundred feet of the rim, we were all exhausted. My constant post-holing the virgin snow, now about 8" above my knees, had slowed me to the point where I told my son I couldn't go any further. I fell back into the snow, unable to do anything except rest. We all rested for a few minutes and once again resumed our trek. Remarkably, the boys had never really complained or said they couldn't go any further–as I had. Some of them showed early signs of frostbite on their hands, but we were able to put more dry socks and clothes onto them. I realized I needed to muster the strength to get all of us to our vehicles before nightfall. There was at least one more "*I can't go any further*" moment for me, but Brian was the one telling me I could do it and that everyone was counting on me to get them to safety. He showed remarkable stamina and maturity in the face of imminent danger, and his encouragement and determination left a lifelong impact on me.

During the final 200 vertical feet, the trail was completely covered. The snow had been blowing sideways into the cliff face all day and had plastered everything in its path. Eventually, we could see the rim and the short, stone wall surrounding the parking lot. We pretty much climbed straight up, all bent over with our hands clawing the snow for handholds, knowing we were going to make it out at last, and with an hour of gloomy February daylight to spare.

    We discovered my Toyota 4-Runner under a snow drift that covered the back and left sides to the roof. I kicked away snow from the exhaust pipe, entered through the right side and started the engine. The boys all piled in as we waited for the engine to warm up and the heater to begin working its magic on our ears, fingers, toes and attitudes. I found my emergency CB radio, put the antenna on the roof, and began calling for help. I didn't own a cell phone back then, but someone eventually responded to my distress calls. It was a fire department somewhere on or near the Navajo Reservation. They said they would immediately contact the National Park Service who would send help.

    After a few minutes, I left my vehicle and went to the stone wall to see if I could spot the rest of our group still below the rim. It was the highlight of an otherwise miserable trip to eventually see them, one by one, climbing on their hands and knees in our tracks up the snowy cliff and over the wall. In the growing darkness, we all finally realized we were united once again and we would soon be warm, dry and safe.

    It wasn't long before a government vehicle parked behind my 4Runner and a national park ranger approached my window. I had never been so happy to see a law enforcement officer in my life! She asked me to get into her vehicle and provide an assessment of the situation. As I entered the passenger side, I noticed a large caliber rifle mounted vertically between the two front seats. This was serious business! I described what we had been through and, more importantly, told her there was another separate group of three people who were unable to hike out and would need rescue. The man from that group had told me he didn't have a backcountry permit to camp, and that the rest of his family was staying in a hotel on the South Rim. While the ranger contacted Search and Rescue, I returned to the boys still thawing out in my vehicle.

By this time it was dark, and I soon saw another set of headlights arriving through the snowstorm. It was a Jeep driven by a Search and Rescue ranger. He quietly spoke with the park ranger and then approached me with a topographic map. We spread the map on the hood and, in the light of our headlamps, I described for the two rangers exactly where the shallow mine shaft was that I had told the group to evacuate to. The shaft is only about 12 feet deep, but would be like a luxury hotel compared to the snowy and windy hilltop they were camped on. Within minutes, the Search and Rescue ranger attached his wooden snowshoes, donned a backpack larger than any I have ever carried, turned on his headlamp and began descending the trail into the dark snowy abyss. I thought to myself, *"Where do they get people like this?"* As it turned out, his stay with the rescued party was much longer than anticipated, and the helicopter rescue was significantly delayed due to strong winds and poor visibility.

When the ranger allowed us to depart the trailhead, I consulted with the other leaders. They had all successfully started their vehicles and were warming their own passengers. I asked them to follow me to the small town of Tusayan a mile beyond the south park entrance. Over my years of hiking the South Rim trails, I had made a habit of staying at the Grand Canyon Squire Inn. It has a couple of nice restaurants, a friendly bar, a small bowling alley in the basement and, most importantly, a Jacuzzi that could probably seat an entire baseball team.

As we left the trailhead parking lot, we were once again cutting new tracks in the snow. There was one large bump of snow left in the parking lot, which I assumed was the vehicle belonging to the three people stranded on the plateau below. The snow was higher than the top of my tires, but the 4-wheel drive worked well and our small procession of trucks and SUV's made a slow and uneventful trip to Tusayan.

I left my vehicle running in the hotel parking lot and approached the front desk. I hadn't seen any other cars or trucks on the road in Tusayan and I noticed the lobby was pretty much deserted, as well. With a sense of urgency I told the front desk agent *"We have 12 people, including 8 young Boy Scouts. We were caught in the snowstorm down in the Canyon and need to get them into the Jacuzzi. We also need rooms for the night, and each boy needs to phone his parents as quickly as possible."* The hotel manager arrived and said he would help us. Most of the day's reservations had been canceled because of poor driving conditions, so they had plenty of rooms available. I returned to our group and we quickly unloaded soaking wet backpacks, and equally soaked-but smiling boys and adults. We would be safe, warm and well fed tonight!

We received a block of rooms and assigned people to each room. Each leader was responsible for making sure everyone in their room got into the Jacuzzi as quickly as possible. This turned out to be an easy task since the boys pretty much ran in the hallways toward the warm water. I returned to the front desk and was surprised to learn that the hotel was giving each of the boys a disposable camera and that our rooms were discounted, as well. After everyone made calls home, we met in the café for much-deserved hamburgers, sandwiches and ice cream. It was great to watch everyone eat the equivalent of breakfast, lunch, dinner and dessert in one sitting. However, it was also sobering to watch the snow still falling from the comfort of our hotel. I couldn't stop thinking about the three people still on Horseshoe Mesa. I hoped that the Search and Rescue ranger would be able to locate them in the snowy storm that we now seemed so far removed from.

After a hearty breakfast, and an equally hearty thank you to the hotel, we departed Tusayan for home. The 250-mile drive was, of course, slower than normal because of the driving conditions. The snow had finally tapered off sometime during the night and, although it was a scenic trip, I had to remain in 4-wheel drive all the way to Black Canyon City, a mere 50 miles from home.

We arrived safely back to our homes and families late Sunday afternoon, and I'm sure the boys had interesting stories and perspectives on what they had been through. The parents of one of the boys on the trip were good friends and neighbors of ours. They stopped by our house a couple of hours after we had arrived home. They brought a fine bottle of whisky for me, and tearfully told me I had probably saved their son's life. I don't know about that, but it certainly seemed like it at the time.

I received a mid-week phone call from the Park Service that the Search and Rescue ranger had successfully found the group I sent him in for. I also found out that it was two days before the weather at the Canyon cleared enough to safely deploy the Park Service helicopter to rescue the group.

The experience affected me more than I would have expected. It was at least two years before I returned to the Grand Canyon. For someone who made 5-10 inner canyon trips a year, my two-year hiatus was like a prison sentence I didn't deserve. On future backpacking trips, I found myself much more anxious and overly cautious, even in mild weather situations. I would wake up several times during the night to check the sky for approaching storms. Eventually, I made a very enjoyable day trip down the Grandview Trail to Horseshoe Mesa with my wife. I showed her where we had camped and where the abandoned mine shaft was. We sat on the edge of a 1,000' cliff, drank a little wine, watched the occasional passing of rafting groups below, and celebrated our twenty third anniversary. I was back!

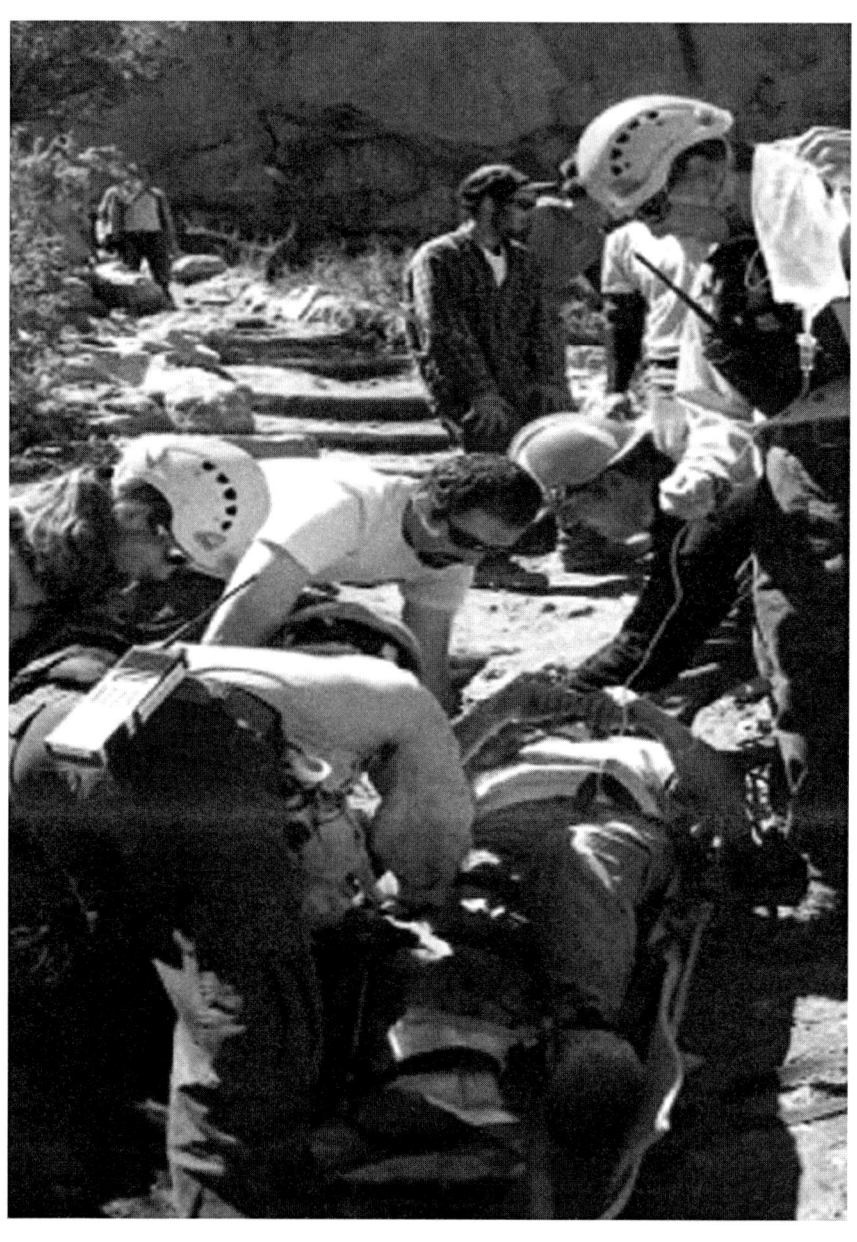

¹ *PSAR team aiding a hiker on the Bright Angel Trail. Photo credit - Canyon Views, grandcanyon.org; Volume XX, No. 1, Winter 2013.*

CHAPTER FOUR

A Day Hike to Prove a Point to Myself

Sometimes you find yourself in the middle of nowhere, and sometimes in the middle of nowhere, you find yourself.
author unknown

I hate to admit it, but my beloved Grand Canyon can be two-faced. For tourists visiting established rim viewpoints and facilities, the stark beauty and vastness certainly rivals any other place on earth. However, for the unprepared hiker or new explorer the Canyon has an insidious side, too. The vastness of the Grand Canyon, especially when viewed from the rim, often plays tricks with the viewer's mind and judgment. Distances that appear to be short or achievable usually turn out to be much longer and harder than anticipated. Many a tourist at the South Rim has spotted the greenery of Indian Gardens below them and determined it is close enough for a quick day hike. The initial downhill hike, although 4.7 miles long, is assisted by gravity and a visitor's sense of adventure for what's around the next bend. However, a wake-up call often occurs when tired hikers must trek the same distance back to the rim while fighting aches and pains and gravity. Nine and a half miles in one day, with a total elevation loss and gain of 6100', is not an easy task for most people. What appears to be so close and so do-able from above can turn into a huge, and sometimes deadly mistake, for many would-be hikers.

To help prevent some of the unfortunate mistakes well-intended hikers sometimes make, the Park Service has an effective Preventive Search and Rescue (PSAR) program in-place.[1] During peak hiking months, it's common to encounter a uniformed PSAR volunteer a mile or two down the Bright Angel or South Kaibab trails. They politely wave, and often ask how you are doing and where you are planning to go. As you respond, they silently assess how you look and how you are dressed, and will engage you in casual conversation until they have drawn a conclusion. Occasionally, they will suggest a shorter route or perhaps a two-hour rest during the heat of the day before you begin your return hike. Most people have a hiking plan and adequate supplies and stamina, but not everyone.

On a beautiful early Saturday morning in September 2013, I decided to take a solo day hike down the South Kaibab, across the Tonto Plateau and up the Bright Angel Trail. This was a personal test for me and I needed to be alone.

It had been exactly two years since a botched emergency surgery to remove my gallbladder had nearly killed me. Due to undiagnosed bile leakage from the surgery I went into sepsis, AFIB and other complications as my body began to shut down. My daughter, Rachael, an excellent nurse at Mayo Hospital, recommended a nuclear HIDA Scan to determine if bile leakage was present. However, the doctor who had performed my surgery insisted there could not be any leakage and wouldn't authorize the costly test. Thankfully, Rachael can be as stubborn as a Grand Canyon mule with a 300-pound passenger if she believes she is right. In this case her persistence prevailed and her recommendation was correct. The test showed significant amounts of bile in my chest cavity. My doctor subsequently, and sheepishly, confessed that my gallbladder had burst as she was trying to remove it via an orthoscopic procedure. She thought she had been able to mop up all the caustic bile but, unfortunately for me, she was very wrong. I was in the hospital for nine days and missed eight weeks of work. Even worse than that, I had a very valid concern that my hiking days might be over. Usually I hike to see the fantastic views. However, today's hike was to get a view of myself. I intended to find out for myself if I could still hike the Canyon. I was mentally prepared, but was I physically ready?

I set a very enjoyable pace of about four miles per hour as I hiked downhill in the early morning daybreak. Somewhere near the Cedar Ridge area I noticed a park ranger walking uphill toward me. I stopped to chat with her for a few minutes, which is a common courtesy in the back country, and told her I was a Wilderness First Responder–a required courtesy. She immediately explained that she could use my help further down the trail.

A few miles below us the ranger had encountered a group of five people hiking out of Phantom Ranch with little or no remaining water. Two were adults and the others were teenagers, and she relayed their circumstances. The group had hiked down the South Kaibab on Friday afternoon intending to stay in the dormitory housing or maybe a cabin. They didn't arrive at Phantom Ranch until well after sunset. However, they had not made reservations in advance and there was no room for them to spend the night. At some time during the night, they had departed Phantom Ranch and started the long, waterless, seven-mile hike back up the South Kaibab Trail. When she came across the group, the two adults seemed to be doing OK but the teenagers were lagging behind and were out of water. The ranger had shared what water she could spare and asked how much I had and if I could share some, as well. I was carrying four quarts, plus I had slowly consumed a quart of electrolytes during the pre-dawn shuttle bus ride to fill my internal canteen. I told her I could offer at least two quarts to the group.

We parted ways after our brief discussion, and it wasn't more than 30-45 minutes before I came across the two adults steadily making their way through the Redwall. I was surprised they had left the three teenagers alone and quite a bit behind. The trail was pretty much a straight line at that point, so I had a couple of minutes to observe how they were doing as our distance closed. I explained that I was a certified emergency responder and asked if they had any food or water with them. I didn't mention my earlier discussion with the ranger. They had no food, and I could see each of them had about a pint of water left in the Gatorade bottles they were carrying. They readily accepted two of my most favorite Clif Bars (Cool Mint Chocolate) but would not take any water. I took some comfort knowing that it had rained a lot in the days prior to this hike. There were water pockets in the rocks higher up the trail that they would encounter, and could drink from, if they became desperate.

As I continued my enjoyable downward descent, it was another 20 minutes before I came across the three teenagers-one male and two females. All of them had obvious weight issues. They were sitting in the sun on rocks just off the trail. As before, I didn't mention any prior knowledge about them. I struck up a conversation, told them they had several uphill miles yet to go, and that I had noticed their small, 16 ounce water bottles were clearly empty. I explained that I had plenty of extra food and water I didn't need to carry and that I was glad to share. I also told them I needed to be assured they were OK before I left them, so I asked them to perform a quick and simple skin turgor test (pinching the skin on the top of their hand to assess a level of dehydration based on how long the skin remains elevated). None of them showed any significant or late-stage dehydration, but I left them three quarts of water, three Clif bars and several hard candies. As I departed, I mentioned there was some fine shade just a few minutes further up the trail. They were nearly up the Tapeats Sandstone layer and would soon arrive at the Tonto Plateau. They would have a great view of the river and how far they had hiked. Unfortunately, they had only hiked a little more than two miles and still had nearly five more to go in full sun, and it was getting hotter by the minute.

Back on the trail once again, I couldn't get their unfortunate, and completely preventable, situation out of my mind. Similar scenarios play out, with varying consequences, in the Grand Canyon nearly every day. The hike down to Phantom Ranch via the South Kaibab Trail is a long, steep and waterless seven miles, and the elevation loss is 4,810 feet–nearly a mile. These five tired and out-of-shape hikers were now trying to make the return hike on inadequate food, water, and rest. Their total trip would be fourteen miles with an elevation loss and gain of 9,620 feet. Despite best efforts by the National Park Service, including large warning signs, messages in the park newspaper, and PSAR volunteers on the heavily used trails, it's difficult to imbue common sense and caution into some people.

If you are this far in the book, you certainly recognize there are very real and inherent risks associated with hiking the Grand Canyon. Would-be hikers with little or no outdoor experience often encounter problems due to the ankle-twisting terrain, different climates, high altitudes, lack of advance preparation, poor decisions, risk taking and little, if any, understanding of their own physical limitations and the demands of the Canyon. Problems in the wilderness can lead to potentially serious situations where immediate help is usually not available.

These situations can rapidly escalate in the back country as food and water are depleted, darkness sets in, temperatures drop, confusion sets in, and psychological self-confidence spirals downward. Realization that no emergency call can be made can be emotionally devastating. People not accustomed to being out of cell phone range, or temporarily off the grid, seem to have a knack for putting themselves in harm's way. Ignorance, poor planning, high testosterone levels, and little, if any advance preparation are common themes in far too many Search and Rescue events. Some events turn out to be life-lessons for those who live and learn, while others turn out to be life-ending situations. The impact these events have on families of the victims, and even on rescue personnel, are devastating and, in retrospect, are usually determined to have been 100% preventable with a good dose of common sense. There are more places in the Canyon that have cell service now, but it is not uniformly available even on the main trails

Seemingly minor mistakes or lapses in judgment can be greatly magnified, and sometimes unforgiven, in the Canyon. Forget a flashlight and you might be eating and cleaning your cookware in the dark. Forget matches or a lighter for your stove and you will be dining on cold, dehydrated meals. Trip on a shoelace and you might fall or sprain your ankle. Lose or clog your water filtration system and you may experience the cleansing properties of my least favorite micro-organisms; Giardia and Cryptosporidium. Forget to pack toilet paper...enough said.

Thorough physical conditioning, good equipment, adequate food and water, self-reliance, and accurate assessment of your limitations are keys to a successful hike. Too often, common sense is replaced by the narrow-minded goal of hiking to the river and back in a day. If you are hiking downhill and think you might be getting tired, turn around and hike uphill for a couple of minutes. If you struggle or are out of breath, your decision to turn around should be easy. Make the right choice. Stop where you are, find shade if you're overheated, rest and re-hydrate, and consider waiting until early evening to hike out. Don't become a statistic or yet another entry in the mounting log book of rescues or deaths.

The remainder of my day hike down the South Kaibab, across the Tonto Plateau to Indian Gardens, and up the Bright Angel, was trouble-free. As I neared the top, the internal celebrations began. My spirit seemed renewed. I was now confident that the grueling effects of my botched surgery wouldn't prevent me from one of the things I loved the most. I would be able to continue taking family and friends on new explorations, and I might just reach my self-imposed goal of "400 Days in the Grand Canyon" I had set for myself many years before. In truth, I had actually set a goal of 365 days, a year in the Grand Canyon, and was up to 378 when surgery interrupted, and nearly ended, my progress. I have promised my wife, my best hiking partner, that we will indeed explore and hike new places. Today, we are hiking many new trails under the Mogollon Rim in the east-central Mountains of Arizona where we live. There is so much more yet to be discovered by us in Arizona and the surrounding western states. I'm pleased to report that new explorations are well underway without any lingering health issues.

North Kaibab Trail. Courtesy of NPS.

CHAPTER FIVE

Rim-to-Rim Logistics and Adventures

Life begins at the end of your comfort zone.
Neale Donald Walsch

For many people, the ultimate Grand Canyon experience is a Rim-to-Rim (R2R) hike. Successful completion of this 23.9-mile trek comes with well- deserved bragging rights and, for many, a chance to accomplish a big Bucket List item. The local gift shops are well stocked with commemorative Rim-to-Rim coffee cups, T-shirts, bumper stickers, hiking stick emblems, and other similar memorabilia to help limping hikers recall why their toenails are coming off.

When I meet new people who hear about my Grand Canyon experiences, a very predictable first question is often, *"Have you done Rim-to-Rim?"* In our goal-oriented society, the R2R experience has come to define the way many hikers choose to experience the canyon. First time visitors to the North or South rims often decide to someday return and hike R2R. Most of them take the necessary steps to prepare for the trip but, of course, some have a better experience than others do.

Two well-maintained trails in the popular Grand Canyon corridor area provide easy, but not full-year, access for R2R hiking. The North Kaibab Trail and the Bright Angel Trail meet at the Silver Bridge. The bridge is one of two long and narrow suspension bridges that span the Colorado River near Phantom Ranch. The North Kaibab Trail begins at the North Rim and twists, turns and drops about 6,000' over its 14.5-mile maintained route to the bridge. Similarly, the Bright Angel Trail departs the heavily visited South Rim and drops about 5,000' over 9.4 miles to meet up with its northerly trail partner at the bridge. Together, they offer a relatively convenient, but often difficult route to experience some of the best attractions nature has to offer in this section of the Grand Canyon.

With careful planning and preparation, the R2R trek can be a true experience of a lifetime. A successful trip of this nature requires thorough attention to logistics, permits, weather forecasts, food, equipment, hydration, clothing, footwear and personal readiness. The vast difference in altitude and climate between the North Rim and the Colorado River means that hikers will walk through five unique climate zones (Hudsonian, Canadian, Transition, Upper Sonoran and Lower Sonoran zones). Looked at another way, a hike from the North Rim to the Colorado River is equivalent to hiking in climates from Southern Canada to Northern Mexico.[1]

There are numerous logistical options to consider when planning a R2R hike. Although this is not a comprehensive "How to Hike the Canyon" book, my conscience and life-experiences lead me to inform readers of a few basic things that potential R2R hikers should be aware of.

The North Rim is at least 1000' higher than the South Rim, so most R2R hikers elect to descend the North Rim and hike up to and out via the South Rim. Beginning your hike on one side of the Canyon, and finishing on the other side, can mean the vehicle you drove to the Canyon is a long way away! To avoid this situation, many hikers park their vehicle at the South Rim and arrange transportation in advance via the Trans Canyon Shuttle (www.trans-canyonshuttle.com). The shuttle operates mid-May through mid-October and is a great way to move you and your equipment, as well as make new hiking friends. The trip typically takes five to six hours and is 210 miles long. I have used this service many times and have always had excellent, safe, and friendly drivers. Remember, too, that the trailhead for the North Kaibab Trail is a one-mile hike from the campground or the North Rim Lodge. The lodge offers a Kaibab trailhead shuttle twice daily, and reservations need to be booked with the front desk at least one day in advance.

If your R2R hiking group is large enough, and you trust someone else to drive that new sports car of yours, you can consider splitting into two smaller groups. One group would take transportation from the South Rim to the North Rim, and the remaining group would overnight at the South Rim. Both groups would begin their hike the following morning and then meet-up along the trail to exchange car keys. Be sure to tell the party receiving your keys exactly where you parked your car. I seem to recall spending most of an afternoon wandering around the parking lot near the train depot trying to locate my friend's car.

Hikers intending to do R2R in one day do not need a backcountry permit from the National Park Service. Hikers doing R2R and staying in the dormitories or cabins at Phantom Ranch also do not need backcountry permits but must have advance reservations. Reservations for cabins or dormitories at Phantom Ranch are *extremely* limited and difficult to obtain. Hikers intending to stay in any campgrounds below the rims (i.e. Indian Gardens, Bright Angel, Cottonwood), or intending to camp at large in designated areas, must apply for and receive a backcountry permit prior to their hike. While a very small number of permits are available at the Backcountry Information Center (at both the South and North rims) on a walk-up basis, most permits are issued via a fax system. Applicants can fax a written permit request as early as the first of the month, four months before the proposed start month. Verbal and in-person permit requests are only possible for hike dates one to three months out. If this seems confusing, which it can certainly seem, consult the National Park Service's very comprehensive website.[2]

Many people are quite surprised to learn that it snows in Arizona. And, it can really snow at the North Rim! In fact, measurable snow has been recorded at the North Rim in every month of the year. According to the National Park Service, average yearly snowfall at the North Rim is 142 inches with a record snowfall of 272.8 inches.[3] For comparison purposes, Anchorage, Alaska receives an average annual snowfall of 73 inches with a record annual snowfall of 133 inches. For this reason, the North Rim is closed from mid-October to mid-May. State Highway 67 is the beautiful and very scenic road that leads to the Grand Canyon North Rim entrance, and it closes each year just beyond the Jacob's Lake Inn. On rare occasions, there will be sufficient snow to impact driving even earlier than the typical mid-October closing. Potential R2R hikers should call Arizona Highway Information at (888) 411-7623 in advance of their trip if cold or uncertain weather conditions could be a concern.

One particularly memorable trip provides a real example of the North Rim's unpredictable weather. During a late September trip to Thunder River with a few hiking buddies, we experienced a surprise snowstorm that had not been predicted. We were on our way to Crazy Jug Point to spend the night before hiking to Thunder River. As we parked our cars at the Jacob Lake Inn for dinner, we were treated to quite a lightening show but no precipitation. During a quick dinner at the counter, a man came in with snow on the shoulders of his jacket. We were surprised since it had been cloudy but not snowing just a half hour before. I quickly rented the last cabin they had available, and our group enjoyed watching *Blazing Saddles* while it lightly snowed.

By morning's first light, the road to the North Rim was dusted with snow but it was not closed. There were no vehicle tracks on the road as we departed the Inn. We had driven only a few minutes when we saw a turkey vulture in the middle of the snowy road. It was picking away at some sort of roadkill. My friend, Pruitt, driving the car ahead of me, rolled down his window and motioned for me to slow down and stop. I was shocked that we were about fifty feet from a large mountain lion just off the left side of the road. The lion was very slowly sneaking up on the unwitting and hungry vulture enjoying his breakfast. We quickly shut our cars off and watched nature unfold in front of us. Once the mountain lion thought he was close enough, he sprang through the air in an attempt to grab the vulture. He didn't succeed, but his gracefulness and ability to leap fifteen feet or so were something I will never forget. How *could* I forget? Snow lightly falling, prospects of a great hike to my favorite place, a night time of fine cultural entertainment, time with my son and best buddies, and witnessing an early morning show that any wildlife photographer would be proud to capture.

Now that the backcountry permit, transportation and lodging issues are taken care of, it's time to discuss a few unique things to see and do on the hike from the North Rim to Phantom Ranch and the Colorado River:

The North Kaibab Trail, constructed in 1927 to replace a former Indian and prospector route, is one of the most beautiful hikes in the Grand Canyon. Of the three regularly maintained trails in the park, it is the least visited and the most difficult. The trail begins at an elevation of 8,241' and quickly descends the Muav and Redwall formations. The trail itself was blasted from the canyon walls and offers stunning views and breathtaking drop-offs. Bright Angel Canyon offers considerable morning and late afternoon shade, which is welcome in the summer, but it can be very cold and often wet or frozen in the shoulder seasons.

As Bright Angel Canyon begins to open up, you will first hear, and then see, Roaring Springs on your left at mile 4.7. The spring is fed by the Redwall aquifer approximately 3,800 feet below the North Rim. There is a water pipe inserted into a deep pool inside Roaring Springs that extracts the pure, limestone-filtered water. Some of this water is pumped upward to the North Rim, the South Rim, and to Desert View on the East Rim. The rest of the water becomes Bright Angel Creek. The aluminum water pipeline is occasionally viewable during the hike to Phantom Ranch. It is buried under the trail and parallels Bright Angel Creek, crosses the creek six times, hangs onto the underside of the silver suspension bridge, and heads toward Plateau Point where water is thrust uphill about 1,300' to Indian Gardens. Large, well-hidden pumps at Indian Gardens make a final push up an additional 3,800', and the Roaring Springs water arrives at the South Rim where it is stored for use by nearly 5,000,000 visitors a year.

The sixteen-mile Trans-Canyon Pipeline from Roaring Springs to the South Rim has a fascinating history. It was a true engineering feat, and was one of the most complex and dangerous projects ever undertaken in a national park. In 1963, the pipeline contract was the largest contract the National Park Service had ever awarded. Workers toiled from 1963 to 1965 to fabricate and place the custom-built and hand-fabricated water pipeline. By early December, 1965, it was nearing completion. However, on December 5, 1965, it began to rain. And rain some more. The rain continued for a day and a half. When the massive 1,500-year flood began to subside, eighteen inches of rain had fallen on the rocky watershed that drains into Bright Angel Creek. The engorged creek–now a river–flowed through narrow Bright Angel Canyon at 20'-30' high. It easily swept boulders the size of automobiles into the newly installed and nearly completed pipeline. Every piece of equipment, including Caterpillar tractors and construction trucks, was gone and presumably swept through Bright Angel Canyon and into the Colorado River. The flash flood tore out 8.5 miles of the new 9-mile pipeline. After a year of legal wrangling, the government resumed funding for the water pipeline, and it was successfully completed in 1967. Today, the pipeline is two decades beyond its anticipated life expectancy and, with frequent repairs and tender loving care, continues to deliver an average of 500,000 gallons of water each day. The project remains the largest helicopter-supported construction project ever completed in the United States, and required more than 25,000 helicopter flight hours.[4]

After hiking 2.1 miles beyond Roaring Springs you will come to Cottonwood Campground. This campground, built in the 1920s and improved and modernized in the 1930s by the Civilian Conservation Corps, is the most rural of the three campgrounds on the R2R trails, but is still well equipped. There are 11 campsites that will accommodate six people, and one larger campsite designated for 7-11 people. The campground is equipped with treated drinking water, picnic tables, metal bars to hang backpacks, and metal ammunition boxes for rodent-resistant food storage. There are also composting toilets, a ranger station/residence, bulletin board and emergency phone. Note that the ranger station is not staffed at all times. It's possible that a ranger will not be available if one is needed. However, there are rangers located at Phantom Ranch and also at the Roaring Springs maintenance residence.

Even though I don't typically camp at Cottonwood, I have had two interesting experiences there. During a R2R hike in October 2005, my wife and I hiked into Cottonwood campground where we noticed several people sitting on top of picnic tables in a large, shaded area. Curiosity got the better of us and we walked over to see what the group was doing. What we saw was amazing! Everyone on the picnic tables had their feet up on the tables as well, and for good reason. As strange as this might sound, we watched a pink, Grand Canyon rattlesnake and a wild turkey having a life-or-death fight. Each time the rattlesnake would strike, the turkey would jump into the air to avoid being bitten. When the turkey landed, it would immediately sneak up behind the snake and bite it behind the head. This would, of course, provoke the snake again and the process repeated itself. It reminded me of watching the Congress and Senate bicker at each other on C-SPAN. After watching for perhaps five minutes, the two fighters must have declared a truce. The snake slithered under some bushes, and the turkey proudly walked back up the trail and out of sight on its way toward Roaring Springs. Try as I might, I just couldn't make this story up!

The other interesting experience occurred during a very rainy and cold R2R hike. As we slogged through the red mud past Cottonwood, our progress toward Phantom Ranch was briefly halted by the local ranger. She explained that a side canyon just down the trail a bit near Hattan Butte had flashed (Canyon-speak for a flash flood) and was still running too high for hikers to safely cross through.

During this time, while a dozen of us waited patiently in the rain, the ranger told us that less than an hour earlier a hiker had insisted she pass through instead of waiting for the flooding to subside. She told the ranger she was a financial executive and needed to maintain her tight schedule in order to return to Phoenix for an important meeting. Although the ranger tried to stop her, the hiker began to wade through the flash flood. She was knocked off her feet and swept into Bright Angel Creek. Fortunately for her, Bright Angel Creek was not at flood stage yet and she was able to make her way to shore, wet and bruised and humbled by her arrogance and inexperience. And, I hope she was late for her meeting.

A must-see feature of the R2R experience is Ribbon Falls. Located 1.6 miles past Cottonwood Campground on creek-right as you hike south, it is a 15-20 minute hike off the main Bright Angel Trail. The small falls is located in a side canyon and flows year-round. The water comes from a spring several hundred feet higher up the cliff face. Over the eons, the steady flow of water has deposited minerals, which have built up a table-shaped, mossy, calcium carbonate dome several feet high. Ribbon Falls was originally named "Altar Falls" due to the altar-like rock that the steady falls continues to build. During hot weather, Ribbon Falls is a great place to relax and wait out the heat. It's easily day-hiked from Cottonwood Campground (3.2 miles round trip) or from Phantom Ranch or Bright Angel Campground (approximately twelve miles round trip). It is interesting to note that the Zuni Indians, now of western New Mexico, consider the falls to be their mythological place of origin. The falls is occasionally closed for a day by the Park Service so that the Zunis can visit their sacred spiritual site.

Back on the trail once again, you will notice Bright Angel Canyon narrowing and closing in on you. This area is known as "The Box" and is in the Vishnu Schist layer, some of the oldest exposed rock (1.8 billion years) in the world. The rock is mostly black and pink. It quickly absorbs heat during the day and is slow to cool down in the evenings. As you approach Phantom Ranch, the canyon widens once again. You've made it!

Phantom Ranch was designed by famous architect Mary Coulter, and was completed in the early 1920s. There are many well written and comprehensive books and on-line reference materials that explain the history, facilities, climate, and lodging/reservations process. Therefore, I will only provide some tidbits I would want to know if I was a first-time hiker headed to Phantom Ranch:

There are lots of great day hikes in the area. Staff members are always willing to offer their advice on their favorite hiking spots.

One of my favorite things to do is to stretch out on the nearby Black Bridge in the dark and look at the stars. On moonlit nights, the river reflects like a mirror. On moonless nights, it's fun to look for the International Space Station as it slowly arcs across the sky like a slow moving star. Sometimes, you might even see hiker's headlamps as they carefully make their way in the dark down the switchbacks toward Phantom Ranch.

Write a post card to friends or family. Cards and letters can be hand-stamped "*Mailed by Mule from the Bottom of the Grand Canyon*" and carried out of the canyon by mule each day. Don't forget to bring addresses with you. Post cards and stamps are available in the canteen.

Hikers and mule riders journey to Phantom Ranch from all over the world. Visit the canteen after breakfast, at lunchtime or after dinner, and take time to meet someone new. Enjoy a cold lemonade, a glass of wine, or a beer while you are there.

Purchase a Phantom Ranch T-shirt at the canteen. The design changes each year, and the shirts are not available anywhere else.

If you're staying in a dormitory or cabin, hot showers, soap, shampoo and towels are provided, as is your bedding. Did I mention hot showers?

Bring a credit card. Cash is, of course, accepted too, but I find a credit card is easier. If you use money, leave your change in the tip jar. Loose change gets heavy when you have to carry it a vertical mile out of the canyon.

Pull up a rock and put your feet in the creek. After all, you'd pay a lot for such relaxing, remote and stunning scenery at a spa somewhere.

Take the self-guided walking tour to learn about the history and the people of Phantom Ranch. Ask a staff member to show you where the swimming pool used to be. Really!

Walk down to the boater's beach and put your feet in the river. Colorado River water comes out of the bottom of Glen Canyon Dam at an average temperature of 46 degrees most of the year. However, don't go past your knees and *absolutely do not try to swim!* The cold water can quickly lead to hypothermia (see Chapter 10 for more details on this phenomenon).

When you are ready to depart Phantom Ranch for the South Rim, you have two trail choices—the South Kaibab Trail, which begins at the Black Bridge, or the Bright Angel Trail, which is accessed via (but doesn't actually begin at) the Silver Bridge. Hikers wanting to take the Bright Angel Trail must first cross the Silver Bridge and hike 1.7 miles on the River Trail, which connects to the Bright Angel at Horn Creek. The Bright Angel and South Kaibab trails both have their advantages and disadvantages.

The South Kaibab Trail[6]

The South Kaibab is the lesser traveled of the two trails to the South Rim from Phantom Ranch. It is well engineered and maintained, as trails go, and the route is straightforward and easy to follow. Compared to the Bright Angel, it is shorter, steeper and hotter, and has no water.

The South Kaibab was built by the National Park Service in 1924-1925 as an alternate to the Bright Angel. An early Grand Canyon pioneer, Ralph Cameron, controlled the Bright Angel Trail and charged hikers a $1 toll to use it. The National Park Service, which took control of Grand Canyon in 1919, attempted to purchase the trail rights from Mr. Cameron, but his asking price of $150,000 was too high for the Park Service. Instead, the Park Service decided to design and build its own trail at a cost estimated at $40,000. The trail was engineered to be 4' wide; 6.5 miles long (to the river) and have a maximum grade of 18%. The trail was intended to be used all-year-long by mule trains servicing Phantom Ranch. Unlike most other Grand Canyon trails, it was constructed on a ridge line rather than in a canyon or following a fault line. To assure year-around availability, even in the cold and snowy winter season, it was designed to be fully exposed to the sun. In fact, only a quarter-mile of the trail is *not* in the full sun.

When the South Kaibab was completed in 1925 (at a final price of $73,000) it was initially named the Yaqui Trail since it began at Yaqui Point. However, it was re-named Kaibab; a Paiute term meaning "mountain lying down." One of the first uses of the new trail was for transportation of the steel cables for the Kaibab suspension bridge across the Colorado River. It must have been quite a sight to see 42 Havasupai Indians laboring to carry eight steel cables, one-at-a-time, to the bottom of the Grand Canyon. Each cable was 550' long, 1.5" in diameter and weighed 2,320 pounds.[5] My rudimentary math skills tell me that each man had to shoulder about 55 pounds. At least it was a downhill effort. The last time I was in the canteen at Phantom Ranch there was a picture on a wall showing the cables being transported on the shoulders of men much stronger than me.

When making your way up the South Kaibab, you will hike through eight major geologic formations and gain elevation quickly. There is rarely a wasted step on this trail since most of it either goes up or remains level. As compared to the Bright Angel, there are very few spots where you lose the elevation you have worked so hard to gain.

Once you have reached the Tonto Plateau, you are already 1200' above the river at an area known as the "Tipoff." There are composting toilets off the trail to the east, and the small, covered porch is often the only shade in this area. This is also the junction of the Tonto Trail, which runs east and west along the Tonto Plateau. For planning purposes, note there are toilets about three miles further up the trail at Cedar Ridge, which is 2.2 miles from the South Rim.

As you continue uphill from the Tonto Plateau, you might notice the temperature dropping a bit. Typically, the higher you hike the lower the temperature will be. Please note that I *don't* recommend hiking the South Kaibab Trail *uphill* in the hot summer months unless you hike very, very early in the morning or at night.

It's likely you will encounter at least one mule train during your hike out from Phantom Ranch. It is important to know that mules always have the right-of-way on all trails. You are required to step several feet off the trail and, if possible, move to the high side of the trail as the mules pass. Remain quiet so that you don't spook the mules. Camera flashes, opening of wrapped snacks, and hiking poles clattering on rocks can easily frighten a mule.

Views of the Canyon are great on the South Kaibab. To the east you will see Horseshoe Mesa, which is reached by the Grandview Trail. The large drainage between you and Horseshoe Mesa is Cremation Canyon (a personal favorite camping area), which is reached via the lengthy, trans-canyon Tonto Trail. Looking north, you will see Bright Angel Canyon, which is the drainage you hiked down and through from the North Rim to Phantom Ranch and the river crossing. In between Horseshoe Mesa and Bright Angel Canyon are two magnificent peaks-Brahma Temple and Zoroaster Temple. Looking west, parts of the Bright Angel will sometimes come into view as it winds its way upward to the Tonto Plateau. You can see the Devil's Corkscrew, which is a series of steep and difficult switchbacks taking hikers 1200 feet uphill toward Indian Gardens.

After continuing through Skeleton Point, Cedar Ridge, and Ooh Ahh Point, all great rest stops and photo opportunities, you are almost to the top. A narrow series of steep switchbacks tucked into a small canyon, or "chimney" will bring you to the top of the South Rim. You will have hiked uphill nearly a mile (4,850 feet). The lookout point where the South Kaibab Trail begins and ends is Yaqui Point, and transportation is provided by regularly scheduled Park Service shuttle bus. You can sometimes-but not always-find limited trailhead parking close to Yaqui Point on the East Rim Road about 250 yards to the east next to a small picnic area.

If you successfully hike the South Kaibab, congratulations are in order. The trail is generally regarded as more difficult than the Bright Angel.

The Bright Angel Trail[6]

The Bright Angel is the most heavily traveled trail at the Grand Canyon. Curious tourists right off the bus or train, families stretching their travel-weary legs, mule trains with freshly-minted cowboys and cowgirls, and backpackers and hikers of all ages and capabilities use the Bright Angel. As you make your way up the trail, you will encounter more and more people as you get closer to the South Rim. A reliable indication that you are near the top is usually a sighting of a businessman in dusty dress shoes or a woman in high heels.

The geology and history of the Bright Angel are as interesting and varied as the many tourists you will encounter when you make your way toward the South Rim. The trail was constructed to closely follow one of the geologic faults, or cracks, in the Grand Canyon's many layers. The Bright Angel Fault is clearly visible from the South Rim if you know where to look, and evidence of displacement and upheaval are easiest to see from the rim in the lighter-colored layers. A careful observer at Phantom Ranch will note that the layers on the east side of the canyon don't quite match up with the layers on the west side. This is because the west side is 150 feet higher today than when the layers were deposited hundreds of millions of years ago. In fact, the Bright Angel Fault is still busy altering and adjusting the Grand Canyon. Occasionally, visitors and staff at Phantom Ranch will feel a slight movement as the fault makes yet another minor adjustment to reduce built-up stresses along the active fault line.

As you approach the Colorado River from Phantom Ranch, you will take the slightly swaying Silver Bridge. You will quickly find that the floor of the bridge is see-through metal grating. It's interesting to note that the Black Bridge has thick rubber matting on the floor. This is because mules get scared and won't cross a bridge when they can see the flowing river below them. For this reason, all mule trains use the Black Bridge, regardless of which of the two trails they use to access the South Rim.

Once across the Silver Bridge the Bright Angel (referred to in this area as the River Trail) parallels the Colorado River, ascends 550 feet, and then descends once again to 50 feet above river level. There are dunes of wind-blown sand from the nearby river beaches along this section of the trail. After 1.7 miles you will arrive at the Pipe Creek Rest House and the beginning of the Bright Angel Trail. The three rest houses on the Bright Angel were constructed by the Civilian Conservation Core in the 1930s. From this point on, you will depart the river and gain 1200 feet in altitude as you labor up the steep Devil's Corkscrew through the Vishnu Schist layer. The trail continues through the Tapeats Narrows and generally follows Garden Creek toward Indian Gardens.

Upon arrival at Indian Gardens, you will know you are back in civilization once again. This is the first of three locations where you should be able to get drinking water. The pipeline from Roaring Springs, which supplies water to Indian Gardens and the rest houses above, is prone to leaks and breakage from old age, rock slides, freezing, etc. It breaks an average of 5-30 times a year. In fact, as this book is being researched and written, construction is underway on significant repairs and replacement of the half-mile section of the pipeline most prone to breakage. Always check Bright Angel drinking water availability at Phantom Ranch prior to your departure. Also, be aware that the water at 1.5 Mile Rest House and 3 Mile Rest House is shut-off during the winter months due to freezing. However, water is usually available year-around at Indian Gardens. In addition to potable water, there are composting toilets, a very nice campground, mule tie-ups and corral, a staffed ranger station with helipad, an emergency telephone, picnic tables and benches, and lots of shade from old growth Cottonwood trees. There are also lots of squirrels. In fact, one of the most common injuries in the Grand Canyon are fingers bitten by squirrels. Please don't feed them. Indian Gardens is also home to the well disguised and critically important lifting pumps that push the fresh water from Roaring Springs upwards another 3060' to the South Rim. Out of view, too, is the perennial spring that becomes Garden Creek.

Indian Gardens received its name from the early Grand Canyon pioneers who hiked down to the area and observed ancient housing, storage granaries, and evidence of prehistoric farming and agriculture. Native American tribes took advantage of the perennial water from Garden Greek and farmed this small, arable plateau for centuries. In later years the Havasupai farmed the area as well. However, in 1903 President Roosevelt ordered the Havasupai to vacate their native gardens. It wasn't until 1928 that the last of the Havasupai reluctantly made their final hike from their agrarian oasis.

As you depart Indian Gardens, you will hike steadily uphill on the talus slope leading to the South Rim. This section of the trail is straightforward and provides good elevation gain as you approach the steep switchbacks that comprise the remainder of the trail. After hiking 1.6 miles uphill, you will arrive at the Three Mile Rest House. At this point you are 2112' below the South Rim. As mentioned previously, there should be drinking water available in the temperate months. There are also composting toilets, and the rest house provides a little shade, which is welcome in the hot summer months. And, I should add, even more squirrels pretending to be hungry for any extra food that hikers may wish to shed before their final push to the South Rim. Please don't feed them.

At about two miles from the South Rim, you will pass Two Mile Corner where there are some ancient pictographs dated to 1300 A.D. They can be difficult to find, so this is a good area to sit for a few minutes and study the rocks. I typically use just about any excuse, including archeological interest, to rest for a minute or two before making the final push for the top.

The last water stop and bathroom break is at the 1.5 Mile Rest House. At this point, you are 1131' below the South Rim. Many visitors to the South Rim who want to take a leisurely walk into the Grand Canyon use the 1.5 Mile Rest House as their destination and turn-around point. They are the smart ones, especially in the summer months. Many other casual walkers are lulled into thinking that the hiking is easy. They are *going down*, and they are definitely *wrong*.

In 2014 there were 324 Search and Rescue operations conducted by National Park Service Search and Rescue personnel.[7] Many of these were due to dehydration and hyperthermia (overheating) and nearly all were preventable. In fact, as I was writing this chapter in June 2015, a 36-year old male hiker from Japan died from hyperthermia while hiking the Devil's Corkscrew portion of the Bright Angel Trail from the Colorado River. The temperature on the trail was more than 110 degrees, and a heat advisory was in effect. Don't become a statistic. Remember that any trail you hike down when you are fresh, rested, and full of energy must be hiked back up when you are tired, hot, and possibly low on food and water. Remember, too, that most people hike downhill at 2.0-2.5 miles per hour, and most people hike uphill at one mile per hour or less. Never plan to hike rim-to-river and back in one day. The Park Service doesn't even make the mules do that.

The hike from the 1.5 Mile Rest House to the South Rim basically consists of more low-grade switchbacks, occasional train whistles as the Grand Canyon railway arrives and departs, youngsters coyly slipping behind guard rails to take pictures, and freshly showered tourists staring at your sweaty face, your heavy backpack, and your dust-covered socks and boots. Try hard to wipe that smile off your face as you realize you are getting closer and closer to the ice cream shop and the small, cozy bar at the Bright Angel Lodge. Not to mention the gift shops that sell all of the Rim-to-Rim memorabilia? Buy some...you certainly have earned it!

1. Climate data and text from www.summitpost.org and www.wikopedia.org.
2. www.nps.gov/gcra/planyourvisit/backcountry-permit.htm.
3. www.nps/gov/gcra/learn/nature/weather.htm)
4. Water pipeline history from www.helicopterfoundation.org, by Martin Pociask.
5. *The Story of Man at the Grand Canyon*, J. Donald Hughes.
6. Historic and geologic information from *Nature, Culture, History at the Grand Canyon*, Sarah Bohl Gerke, Arizona State University, 2010.
7. www.azcentral.com/story/news/local/...rescues-grandcanyon/28968575.

*Nearing the Top of the South Kaibab Trail.
Note the Mule Riders. Courtesy of NPS.*

CHAPTER SIX

The Powell Plateau: Find your Own Bliss

*There's many a man who never tells his adventures,
for he can't hope to be believed.*
Arthur Conan Doyle

I told my friends, as part of my dialogue to convince them to make yet another adventure with me, something along these lines: "There's this isolated plateau, well off the beaten path, that has steeply terraced, unclimbable slopes on all sides, and is only connected to the North Rim by a small, narrow land bridge. It's just like the fictional plateau in Arthur Conan Doyle's book, The Lost World, except this plateau isn't fiction."

I include this chapter because the Powell Plateau is such a unique, relatively accessible, and fun place to explore. It's a mostly flat table top, about 8.5 miles square, steeped in ancient and recent history. It offers a rare example of an old-growth Ponderosa pine forest undisturbed by modern forestry practices. Often overlooked because of its isolated location off a long unmaintained road in the North Rim back country, it's worth the effort if you are seeking something other than a typical lengthy Rim-to-River hike.

The trailhead is accessed by driving south from Jacob's Lake on Highway 67 for 26.5 miles, and then on various improved, and not-so-improved backcountry roads for another 18 miles to Swamp Point. A high clearance vehicle is necessary-especially for the last 8 miles on Swamp Ridge Road. If it rains during your trip, a four-wheel drive vehicle is essential when negotiating the muddy Swamp Ridge Road back to FS 268B.

A backcountry permit is also required if you intend to spend at least one night on the Powell Plateau. Note also that the North Rim is closed from mid-October to mid-May due to snow and freezing conditions, and Swamp Ridge Road can sometimes be closed until early June while the Forest Service clears the fallen trees from the past winter season. A check with the Forest Service prior to your departure is always advisable whenever traveling on the Kaibab Plateau.

The hike to Powell Plateau is more a brief walk than a true hike for an experienced backpacker. From the North Bass trailhead you will descend 800' during the mile-long, gentle, downhill walk on the limestone switchbacks to Muav Saddle. From here the trail goes left, right, or straight ahead. A left turn leads down the rocky North Bass Trail for fourteen miles to the Colorado River and the historic Bass Camp. Proceeding straight takes hikers 900' up to the top of Powell Plateau. A right turn leads to an unexpected surprise: a small wooden cabin.

In the early years of the 20th century, the U.S. Forest Service was tasked with managing the indigenous wildlife on the Kaibab Plateau. Locals were concerned that there were too many predatory animals, and that the deer population of approximately 4,000, a primary source of meat for the locals, was steadily declining. In 1906, President Theodore Roosevelt established the Grand Canyon National Game Preserve. It encompassed 612,736 acres set aside for protection and propagation of native species. One of its first rulings was to ban the hunting of deer on the plateau. Additionally, large-scale hunting of predatory animals was encouraged. Amazingly, between 1907 and 1939, 816 mountain lions, 20 wolves, 7,388 coyotes and more than 500 bobcats were killed.[1] Not surprisingly, the resulting dearth of natural predators led to an explosion of the deer population, which blossomed to approximately 100,000 animals. Overpopulation subsequently led to over-browsing, which resulted in starvation of much of the herd the government was trying to propagate and protect.

It was during the purge of predatory animals that President Theodore Roosevelt decided to visit the Kaibab Plateau for a cougar hunt. In the early summer of 1913, Roosevelt's representatives assembled a crew of 7 men and 6 pack animals (1 mule, 3 donkeys and 2 horses) and an assortment of hunting hounds. The group was guided by game warden "Uncle" Jim Owens, and they killed three cougars during their hunt. An excerpt from President Roosevelt's personal account of a typical cougar hunt follows:

> *It was a wild sight. The maddened hounds bayed at the foot of the pine. Above them, in the lower branches, stood the big horse-killing cat, the destroyer of the deer, the lord of stealthy murder, facing his doom with a heart both craven and cruel. Almost beneath him the vermilion cliffs fell sheer a thousand feet without a break. Behind him lay the Grand Canyon in its awful and desolate majesty.*[2]

Several years after Roosevelt's hunting escapades, the Park Service built a small, two room rustic cabin where one of Roosevelt's hunting camps had been based. It was named "Teddy's Cabin" in honor of the president who established Grand Canyon National Monument, which eventually became Grand Canyon National Park in 1919. Today, hikers are allowed to spend the night in Teddy's Cabin. It's available on a first-come, first-served basis. There is a small seep known as Muav Spring located 0.2 miles down the North Bass Trail on trail-right. A small cistern contains the slow but reliable seep. As always, filter, treat or sufficiently boil all water prior to drinking.

Several years ago I assembled a group of four hikers: My wife, an excellent hiker in her own right, and two very robust hikers and close friends from my office, Jim and Chuck. I typically aim for a minimum of four people when hiking new or remote locations. In the event someone is injured or needs outside medical attention, one person can stay with the injured party while another person or two hikes out to seek help.

It was mid-September, which, in my mind, is the best time of the year to do most anything on the North Rim. The aspen, maple, birch, and oak trees put on a show of fall colors that rivals anything you will see in the northeastern states. By late September, however, the colors are fading fast and the chance of snow or cold rains increases dramatically.

I'd be negligent if I didn't point out once again the potential for poor weather on the Kaibab Plateau and the North Rim. As mentioned earlier, the area is closed to vehicles from mid-October to mid-May due to winter snow and ice conditions. Many of the poor backcountry road conditions frequently remain well into early summer. June, July and August are sublime with relatively cool temperatures, frequent thunderstorms accompanied by lightening, and the slight but constant threat of forest fires. September is a "shoulder month," which means that winter conditions can supplant summer conditions at any time. Always pay attention to the latest weather forecast, and always keep an eye on the skies. These days, weather is the most significant threat on the Kaibab Plateau. If in doubt, choose the safest option, usually to hike out.

We had an enjoyable downhill hike with our backpacks, which contained food for a two-night stay. Since the hike was so short, and we were celebrating another anniversary together, we opted for a higher level of food versus what we usually brought: Caesar salad, meat-filled tortellini with sauce, chips and salsa, and red wine.

There were no other cars at the trailhead, and we were pleasantly surprised to find Teddy's Cabin unoccupied. The cabin contains two small rooms and several nice, wood-framed windows, which, even at nearly a century in age, manage to keep out the rain. The smallest room is a bedroom with a single-person metal cot without a mattress. The larger room has a single cot as well as a kitchen area with a few built-in shelves. There are also a table and bench, which a couple of people can comfortably sit at. It's a fun place to visit, even if you intend to camp on the plateau. Hang your food when you are away, as the local rodent population likes the cabin, too.

By mid-morning we had set up camp for our two-night stay. We packed lunch and water into our daypacks and made the 900' ascent to the top of the Powell Plateau. The trail is choked in many places with Mexican locust and thorny mountain rose, but the views of the approaching summit offset any temporary inconveniences or leg scratches.

The majestic views from the top of the Powell Plateau are as fine as any in the Grand Canyon. In 1873, Major John Wesley Powell, the Grand Canyon explorer for whom the plateau is named, brought famed artist Thomas Moran to the Powell Plateau. Moran photographed, and subsequently painted "The Chasm of the Colorado," which hung in the halls of the U.S. Capitol building for many decades. In the last 25 years of his life, Moran returned to his place of inspiration, the Grand Canyon, almost yearly. He famously told Congress, *"Of all places on earth, the great canyon of Arizona is the most inspiring in its pictorial possibilities."* [3]

Once you reach the top of the Powell Plateau, you will quickly see how much different it is from the scenery you drove through on your way to the trailhead. Due to its remoteness, the plateau has never been logged for timber or subjected to modern day fire suppression policies. As a result, there are huge ponderosa pine trees, the largest you will likely ever see, scattered throughout the forest. The lower trunks of these majestic pines are scarred and charred by a lifetime of wildland fires, and the understory vegetation is quite healthy and productive. This old growth forest has proven to be resistant to low-intensity fires-primarily caused by lightning-and is extensively studied by forest ecology and wildland fire experts. It is interesting to note that the oldest known ponderosa pine tree in Arizona is estimated to be 1200 years old. [4]

As tempting as it sometimes is to envision ourselves as the first explorers to a new area, the Anasazi clearly beat all of us to the Powell Plateau. In 1978 a physical survey of archaeological evidence was conducted. Approximately 20% of the land was surveyed and the results were staggering: 85 human habitation sites with 195 rooms were located. Estimates for the entire plateau concluded there could have been 316 sites with 700 rooms. Pottery remnants show habitation from AD 1050 to AD 1150. Archaeologists believe the plateau would have supported 200-400 indigenous people, and that migration off the plateau to lower elevations and perennial water sources routinely took place during winter months. [5]

Our group of hikers wasn't interested in searching for archaeological evidence, but it seems likely we must have wandered past many habitation sites. We were, however, interested in the unique views and were not disappointed. Fall at the North Rim usually means controlled burns done by the Forest Service. The distant smoke can be heavy at times, and often obscures the otherwise perfect views. I view these burns as a necessary evil and would much rather endure occasional distant smoky views in return for a healthy and accessible forest.

There is a well-defined trail, leading generally south, that somewhat parallels the east rim of the plateau. Several spurs off the main trail escort you to some awesome lookout points. The views are from east-to-west rather than the more typical south-to-north views you get when visiting the north or south rims. You won't be able to see the Colorado River until you reach Dutton Point. The trail to the point is not difficult but does require crossing through thorny Dutton Canyon. Return the way you came unless you are overnighting on the plateau and intend to head to the western edge the following day.

Our group spent the day exploring the plateau and ending up at Dutton Point. We enjoyed lunch on the East Rim and some of us even napped in the shade of the healthy, old growth forest. We dined in style in the rustic cabin, pumped and purified the spring water, and generally had a wonderful time visiting the Powell Plateau.

There's an old axiom amongst backpackers that goes something like this: *A good trip includes both panic and bliss-you go for the one and learn from the other.* Our trip was all "bliss" and no "panic" and I intend to take more friends on a return visit. I hope you have the opportunity to visit this wonderful and historic destination for yourself. Go find your own "bliss" on the unique Powell Plateau.

1. Young, Chris, *A Texbook History: Use of the Kaibab Lesson in Teaching Biology.*

2, Roosevelt, Theodore *A Book-Lover's Holiday in the Open,* Charles Scribner's Sons, New York. 1916.

3. The American Experience, Public Broadcasting System, Arlington, VA.

4. *Arizona Highways* Magazine, April 2016; Data provided by Wally Covington, Director of the Ecological Restoration Institute at Northern Arizona University.

5. Effland, Trinkle and Euler, *Archaeology of the Powell Plateau: Regional Interaction at the Grand Canyon*, Grand Canyon Natural History Association. 1981.

Teddy's cabin.

South Canyon Trailhead.

CHAPTER SEVEN

A few favorite East Rim Hikes

A year from now what will you wish you had done today?
Anonymous

There are several East Rim-to-River trails that can be hiked, scrambled, and down-climbed with ropes and technical hardware. Soap Creek and South Canyon, two of the three hikes described in this chapter, require some scrambling and route finding, but no real technical climbing experience. They are fun and very different alternatives to the much longer North or South Rim-to-River trails most hikers focus on. These trails give hikers relatively quick access to the Colorado River near Marble Canyon and the Vermilion Cliffs areas. Both hikes require a Grand Canyon backcountry permit if you intend to spend one or more nights. The good news is that permits are typically easy to obtain, as few people seem to do these less popular and very unique hikes. The third trail described in this book, the Spencer Trail, is an uphill day hike from the Colorado River and no permit is required. As an added bonus, the drive between the North and South rims takes you close to several special places that are also worth checking out if you can budget the time. A few of my favorite places are briefly noted in this chapter as well.

Of the several East Rim-to-River hikes I've done, South Canyon and Soap Creek are my favorites. Neither of them is a piece of cake, and both require some degree of route finding and boulder-hopping. As with most canyons in this area, there are tributaries that intersect the main route. Hikers need to have a good map, pay close attention to their return route, and budget adequate food, water, time, and energy. I find that in a group we average about 1.5 miles an hour, either downhill or uphill, in these types of canyons. Plan accordingly because, as they say, your actual mileage may vary!

Northern Arizona slot canyons are dangerous and have the potential for sudden flash flooding. Soap Creek has a few narrow spots, but most of the canyon is wide and more like a desert wash than a narrow canyon. On August 13, 1997, a summer rainstorm developed 15 miles from Antelope Canyon near Page, Arizona, on the Navajo reservation. The canyon is a popular tourist attraction known for its beautiful and twisting vertical walls. Heavy runoff from the distant rainstorm headed downhill toward Lake Mead. Unfortunately, Antelope Canyon was directly in its path. Although skies over the stunning slot canyon were clear, a roaring flash flood quickly filled it with 11 feet of water, tree branches, uprooted cactus, and anything else that could be carried in its deadly, chocolate-colored flow. There were twelve hikers in Antelope Canyon when the sudden and unpredicted disaster struck. Eleven of the twelve were killed and the survivor was fortunate to live:

As the water began subsiding, he said he waded down into the canyon about a mile and found Mr. Quintane being helped by a state trooper. "He was all beat up," Mr. Candelaria said. "He had rolled around a while until he hit a ledge and then pulled himself up. All of his clothes were gone; the water was that strong. It had taken his shoes, his shorts, his shirt, everything. He was just stark naked–bruised and battered. It was horrific, just horrifying to see what it did to him."

A flash flood earlier in the week stranded hundreds of residents and visitors in Havasu Canyon, a tributary gorge of the Grand Canyon. Helicopters evacuated more than 350 residents and 300 tourists from the village of Supai, Arizona.[1]

Always make absolutely certain there is no chance of rain anywhere in your general vicinity prior to, or during your intended hike. The canyons in this area channel run-off from extremely broad geographic areas that are mostly barren of large vegetation. The rocky, sun-baked soil absorbs moisture slowly, so the majority of the rainfall runs downhill into beautiful, narrow drainage canyons, often hundreds of feet deep. The canyons have been etched and incised into the ancient plateaus by these infrequent and sometimes deadly rainstorms and flash floods. The canyons present vivid testimony to the power of rushing water, and are beautiful to explore and enjoy as long as the weather forecast is in agreement.

Soap Creek

Highway 89A (also known as "The Heritage Highway" due to the extensive history in the area) is the scenic road you take to travel between the South and North rims of the Grand Canyon. As you drive west on Highway 89A, the turn-off for the Soap Creek trailhead is 0.2 miles past milepost 548, just past the historic Cliff Dweller's Lodge area. Open the gate and drive southeast 0.1 miles past an old corral and dilapidated line shack. Don't forget to close the gate. Continue east 0.4 miles to the trailhead. There is a large Bureau of Land Management sign announcing "Soap Creek Trailhead." Elevation at this high desert location is 4,197 feet and elevation loss over the 4-mile scramble to the Colorado River is a modest 1,140 feet. Be sure to sign the trail register inside the metal box, and be careful not to let the lid slam down on your hand. Experience taught me this lesson, and a small scar on my right hand is a constant reminder from this very box.

The 4-mile (one way) route through the Soap Creek drainage begins on level, blackbrush-covered ground, and hikers will quickly find they are heading into a deepening and narrowing canyon. During a recent trek a pygmy owl greeted me within the first minute and seemingly intended to be my personal guide. As I hiked closer, it would fly down the canyon a bit and wait for me under a bush. This process repeated itself several times. By the time I could no longer find my avian guide, I was perhaps 15 minutes down the trail and, surprisingly, had descended at least 200' below the desert rim. My volunteer guide must have either assumed I was off to a good start, or didn't want to be responsible for what might happen to me.

The canyon quickly closes in as the route descends, but widens considerably after dropping several hundred feet. Your pace will slow as you encounter countless spots where you will need to sit and slide over smooth pour-offs, or do some old-fashioned route finding for a path that suits your comfort level. New hiking shorts quickly become fashionably well-worn after a visit to Soap Creek. If you encounter muddy areas, which is often the case in the spring or after summer rains, the mud on the soles of your boots will add yet another challenge to your quest for sure footing.

Soap Creek flows into the Colorado River at river mile 11.2 (as measured from Lee's Ferry). Although the river will have dropped approximately 100 feet from Lee's Ferry, the Canyon rim will be more than 1100 feet above you. When you leave your vehicle at the trailhead you will be standing on the Kaibab Limestone layer. As you descend the Soap Creek drainage, you will step back in geologic time through the Toroweap Formation and the Coconino Sandstone before arriving at the Hermit Shale layer and the Colorado River. Once you are at the river, you can hike up the sandy bench above the rapids to view the beginning of the next geologic layer, the sienna-colored Esplanade Sandstone, just downstream of the rapids where the river bends to the left.

There is one particular spot (creek right) where the trail leads to a 10'-12' downclimb. It is easiest negotiated by lowering your backpack and free-climbing or scrambling. There is an alternate, larger dry fall route (creek left) about 50 yards across the canyon to the north. It usually has an old, very worn and weathered rope ladder. I trusted this ladder once, and only once, because the bottom rung splintered when I put my weight on it. On a subsequent trip, I replaced it with an 8' blue nylon webbing ascender, which I attached to an ancient piton at the top. I have not been down Soap Creek since that time so I don't know if my ascender might still be there.

As you get deeper into the canyon it opens up to a much wider expanse, and you will encounter a drainage entering about 90° to your left. Be sure to pay attention to this spot on your return trip, or place a cairn so that you select the correct route back to the trailhead.

Soap Creek never becomes a true sandstone narrows like the famous Paria, Buckskin, or Antelope Canyons. Its true beauty lies in the solitude you will experience in the canyon, and also at the end of the hike when you reach the Colorado River and possibly have the entire area to yourself. Don't be surprised, however, if you encounter a group of river runners enjoying lunch or overnighting on the expansive beach upstream of the rapids a couple of hundred yards. There is plenty of sandy beach for everyone. You will certainly enjoy their company, and their anticipation of what is yet to come for them, as they float toward an adventure of their dreams through Grand Canyon.

A hike into Soap Creek is more a boulder hopping and canyoneering experience than a traditional Grand Canyon trail. While it's possible for a sturdy hiker to make a round-trip hike in one long day, the sandy beach is a fine destination campsite. The loud, raging rapids just downstream are entertaining and fun to witness at river level. I really enjoy this hike, and my leisurely pace brings me to the beach in about three hours. I did a round-trip day hike only once. I don't usually recommend it unless you are pressed for time and have plenty of water, salty food, daylight, and energy.

The hike down Soap Creek is also unique in that it is one of the fastest and easiest ways to get to the Colorado River in minimum time. A very good friend of mine, John Rominek, whom I had previously taken on a hike to Thunder River and Deer Creek, and who successfully rowed an 18' Sotar inflatable through the Grand Canyon on our private river trip, died of cancer several years ago. John had never rowed a river as difficult as the Colorado but, like everything else in his life, he succeeded and never flipped the boat during the 21-day trip. His daughter, a river runner as well, wanted to fulfill John's wishes of having his ashes spread in the Grand Canyon. The Park Service issues special permits for the scattering of human ashes, and regulations stipulate that they can only be spread in undeveloped areas of the park not near any roads, buildings, parking lots, campgrounds, etc.[2] When John's daughter asked where her father's ashes could be spread, I recommended hiking down Soap Creek and having a ceremony at the beach. Unfortunately, I wasn't able to make the hike due to my work schedule. I learned that their trip was somber, and that John's family and friends built a very small driftwood raft on which they placed his ashes. John's final river trip was launched from the quiet beach upstream of the rapids, and he encountered his first and only "flip" in the Grand Canyon as he became one with the wild river he respected and loved so much.

The return hike back to the trailhead follows the same route as your initial hike, but may take longer due to the 1100-foot ascent. At 1.5 miles from the river, there is a small seep at creek right that often has a small amount of water in it if you need it. As mentioned earlier, you will encounter a side canyon intersecting Soap Creek. Pay attention to select the correct path, which, hopefully, you marked with a cairn on your descent. The "incorrect" canyon will also get you out of Soap Creek and onto Highway 89A but it's considerably more difficult and your vehicle will be quite a distance away.

I took my son, Brian, and son-in-law, Justin, down Soap Creek several years ago. They used my trusty Gregory and Arc'Teryx internal frame backpacks, and I defaulted to my aging, but always comfortable, Jansport Rainier external frame backpack. As luck would have it, I broke a pack strap while doing one too many "sit and slide" moves on a large boulder. I always carry a few cable ties (Ty Wraps) with me, and it took three of them to repair my strap. Not more than a half hour later, while twisting and sliding once again, my other pack strap broke. A few more Ty Wraps successfully mended this strap as well. When I returned home, I sent the broken straps, and a photo of my backpack, to Jansport for (hopefully) free replacement. Three decades before, when I purchased my pack, Jansport had advertised a lifetime warranty. A couple of weeks went by and I received an overnight Federal Express box. To my surprise, the box contained a new set of my original pack straps, a set of "new and improved" straps, and a set of "still in development and testing" straps. The box also contained a signed book, *The Hippie Guide to Climbing the Corporate Ladder and Other Mountains: How Jansport Makes it Happen*, by the co-founder of Jansport, Skip Yowell. Talk about customer service! Each of my packs has unique weight and volume characteristics. But, when any of them will do, I still default to my Jansport.

South Canyon

The South Canyon trail (actually, more of a route) is another of the East Rim hikes I especially enjoy, and it's much more challenging than the Soap Creek trail. It is also more remote and not nearly as easily accessed as Soap Creek. The hike requires a lot of boulder hopping and scrambling, but the route is generally straightforward. The best thing about this hike is the unexpected scenery at the end. I recommend South Canyon as an overnight or two, although I have done it as a very long day hike as well. In addition to enjoying the Colorado River, it is possible to hike downstream just a bit to visit beautiful Vasey's Paradise, Stanton's Cave, and some ancient Puebloan dwellings perched well above the river. The sheer Redwall cliff that greets hikers across the river is unique and breathtaking, and is a fun place to shout your name and count how many echoes are returned to you.

The trailhead is reached by traveling west on Highway 89A toward Jacob's Lake and Fredonia, Utah. A high-clearance vehicle is strongly recommended for dirt roads in this area. Turn left onto a maintained dirt road at milepost 559.7. There is a large sign here describing the House Rock Wildlife Area. Be sure to set your trip odometer to "0" before proceeding as mileage noted herein begins at the large sign. Drive this road (marked as 8910) southwest for 10.7 miles until the road splits. Take the left fork and proceed 1.0 mile until you cross a cattle guard and fence. There is a Kaibab National Forest sign near the fence line on the right. Continue straight on 8910 until you are at 19.0 miles on your odometer (you will pass through intersections with FR220 and FR661) and reach the junction of FR632. Turn left at this fork and follow FR632 for an additional 1.9 miles until you arrive at the South Canyon Trail sign. Turn right, cross a cattle guard, and drive 1.0 mile down the increasingly faint strips of road until you reach a small parking area less than 50 feet from the edge of the canyon. The road terminates here, and you will now be able to see South Canyon for the first time. You will see that South Canyon is a nearly straight shot all the way to the Colorado River. Unfortunately, the trail will also appear to be easier than it really is. You will need to negotiate around rocks the size of semi-trucks, but don't be discouraged. The prizes at the end of this trail are worth the effort.

Elevation at the trailhead is 5,600 feet. Elevation at the Colorado River is 2,875 feet for a total descent of 2,725 feet. From the trailhead to the river is 6.5 miles. It is possible to camp at, or close to, the rocky trailhead prior to making your descent. Be aware that there is no water at the trailhead, and there is no reliable water in South Canyon.

Water is, of course, available at the Colorado River. If you are hiking at a very hot time of year, it might be worth taking extra water down with you and stashing it as you go for the second half of the journey up. Also, note that I have never had cell phone reception at this location.

The trail to descend into the canyon can be difficult to find, and is located about 100 yards southwest and downhill of the parking area. Most of this area is exposed limestone, which does not lend itself to distinct trails like dirt does. Look for an old wooden sign on a post (no lettering remains on it), which probably once indicated where the trailhead is. Continue walking downhill past the sign and you should eventually come to a large, 2-foot-tall cairn suggesting where the steep descent begins. There is no marked trail here, but various breaks and chutes in the stone provide a reasonable route. As you descend you will be down-climbing large, weather-worn limestone steps often 10' to 20' or more in height. Take your time, lean in with your pack and body weight toward the cliff face, and pay attention to the best ways to contour your way down toward the floor of the canyon.

This a good time for a few suggestions regarding steep down-hiking. First, always make sure your body's center of gravity is not forward of your feet. Simply stated, don't lean forward when hiking downhill. Your body weight, plus your added pack weight, will likely make you fall forward if your center of gravity isn't at or behind your feet. Second, try not to lock your legs when walking downhill. A slight bend at your knees when landing your foot will prevent adding strong impact pressure to your hip and knee joints. Double check your shoe laces to make sure you can't step on them. Hiking sticks are certainly beneficial, but don't rely on them for your full body weight. I've seen poles break or collapse at the worst possible times, mine included. Finally, take your time, double check hand-holds and foot placement, and focus on what you are doing and not the view below.

After you arrive at the bottom of the drainage, the route gets easier as you bushwhack your way steadily toward the Colorado River. There are a couple of pour-offs that other hikers before you have found routes around and have graciously marked with cairns. Bedrock Canyon eventually intersects South Canyon on the north side and presents a large pour-off. Once again, determined hikers have found and marked a way around this area. A cairned path leads hikers to the right along a lengthy ledge until the trail descends back into the canyon floor. You will continue to encounter smaller drainages entering the main canyon. Again, follow the cairned paths until you eventually reach a rock bench above the river. From here, it is a brief scramble down to the sandy beach and a unique and awesome view of the Colorado River.

The National Park Service summarizes the South Canyon hike quite well as follows:

> *South Canyon is typical of hikes descending off the Marble Bench: steep and loose, minor route finding, lack of meaningful trail, and many miles of ankle-twisting drainage bottom walking. Hikers endure such tribulation so that they may camp along the Colorado River beneath the towering cliffs of the Redwall. Short excursions to the aptly named Vasey's Paradise and the infamous Stanton's Cave are an added benefit and a welcomed reward.*[3]

The sandy beach at South Canyon is popular with river runners, and they typically set up camp by late afternoon at the lower end of the beach. There is plenty of space for hikers and river runners to temporarily co-exist. Find yourself a good campsite at the upper end of the beach, filter the cold river water, and enjoy the scenery you have worked so hard to get to.

Once you have established camp, re-hydrated, and are considering what to do next, take the brief walk downstream to Vasey's Paradise and Stanton's Cave. Vasey's was named by Major John Wesley Powell for his good friend and botanist, Dr. George Vasey. It's a natural groundwater spring in the Redwall formation that has been exposed through river cut erosion. The spring has provided fresh water for humans and flora and fauna for eons. Water comes from three small openings in the steep, rock cliff face and cascades in a broad curtain of rivulets into the Colorado River. Vegetation is typical of most Canyon seeps with maidenhair fern, crimson monkeyflower, and watercress in abundance. Unfortunately, poison ivy is also in abundance. Vasey's is one of only three known areas in Grand Canyon where poison ivy exists.[4]

Stanton's Cave is approximately a half-mile walk downriver from the beach, and is a fine second destination while visiting nearby Vasey's Paradise. The cave is named for Robert Brewster Stanton, one of several men investigating the potential for constructing a railroad through the Grand Canyon. When three men in his party drowned in the river, Stanton gave up his ill-advised railroad dreams, stashed his remaining surveying and camping tools in the cave, and hiked out to Lee's Ferry via South Canyon. As river running and Grand Canyon exploration gained in popularity, more and more people were intrigued by the large, natural cave. Archaeologists excavated the cave in 1969-1970 and their findings were dramatic, More than 60 "split twig" animal figurines dated to 3,000-4,000 years ago, evidence of plants and animals from the Pleistocene era, bones from California Condors, and driftwood that was Carbon 14-dated at 37,000 years old. Today, the cave entrance is fitted with a special gate that allows rare Townsend's big-eared bats to access the cave while keeping curious humans restricted to shining flashlights through the steel bars and wondering what's on the other side.[5]

All good things eventually must come to an end, and so too will your visit to South Canyon. The return hike is essentially the same as the down hike, except that you now must reclaim the 2,725 feet of elevation you lost on your way to the river. Bring lots of water for your return trip, and pay close attention to staying in the main canyon instead of drifting into one of the side canyons by mistake. My first round-trip day hike resulted in running out of water and twisting an ankle. Luckily, it rained just enough to fill some of the rock pockets with water. I drank rain water where I could, and barely had the strength to complete the steep final ascent up the large limestone ridges. Also luckily, my robust friend, Tom, helped me up in a few places. He reminds me today that he will not accompany me if we ever do this hike again unless we include at least an overnight at the beach.

The Soap Creek and South Canyon hikes are not for beginners, or for those who aren't comfortable with routes instead of established trails. They are, however, wonderful opportunities for hikers who have the stamina, equipment, and curiosity to visit remote places not seen by most Canyon hikers. As mentioned, the permits are much easier to obtain, the crowds and infrastructure to cater to them are absent, and the silence and remoteness are unforgettable. Always remember to tell someone exactly where you're going and when you plan to be back out. And, as you make your way back to civilization on Highway 89A, be sure to stop for a great meal or an overnight stay at any of the three unique and historic lodges/restaurants along your route. Here is their contact information:

> Cliff Dweller's Lodge and Restaurant (928) 355-2261 (milepost 547)
>
> Lee's Ferry Lodge and Restaurant (928) 355-2231 (milepost 541.5)
>
> Marble Canyon Lodge and Restaurant (800) 726-1789 (milepost 538.6)

The Spencer Trail

For hikers looking for a relatively short day hike but who don't care for the challenges of hiking Soap Creek or South Canyon, here's another favorite hike. The Spencer Trail begins at the Colorado River at Lee's Ferry and can be done in as little as a half day.

Lee's Ferry is one of my most favorite places in Arizona. It's the launching point for all Grand Canyon river rafting trips, and is also home to the Paria River, the historic Lonely Dell Ranch, the impressive Echo and Vermilion cliffs, Lee's Ferry Historic District (3 preserved buildings and lots of artifacts) and some of the finest cold water trout fishing in North America. It's also one of only two locations in the entire 277-mile Grand Canyon where you can drive to the river (the other being Diamond Creek, which is accessed by Hualapai Tribe permit only). It is also the official northernmost starting point for Grand Canyon National Park.

As you begin the 5-mile drive to the parking area at Lee's Ferry you will encounter signs directing you to a self-serve kiosk on your right. Stop here to purchase the required day-use permit before proceeding to Lees Ferry.

Access to the two-mile (each way) Spencer trail is at the parking lot located at the bustling boat ramp. Grab plenty of water, a hat, sunscreen, snacks, and a camera, and walk the dirt road upriver through the parking lot to the riverside trail. Continue paralleling the river for a quarter-mile or so past a barely visible and sunken wooden steamboat until you see a sign for the Spencer Trail. The trail is easy to follow and brings hikers 1,600' to the top of the Kayenta and Navajo sandstone cliff overlooking Lee's Ferry and the surrounding geologic area. On a clear day I'd bet you can see 100 miles or more. The trail is considered strenuous by the Park Service, and includes a garden variety of steep switchbacks, relatively flat sections, well-constructed steps, and a bit of unprotected exposure just for good measure. All in all, one of my favorite quick hikes, and the 360° views quickly make you forget the effort required to get there.

The Spencer Trail was constructed by Charles H. Spencer and his workers as a burro route to transport coal from Warm Creek, Utah, 28 miles upstream, to Lees Ferry. He intended to operate a steam-powered gold sluicing machine at Lees Ferry and required large amounts of coal for the boilers. Once the trail was completed, Spencer realized the effort required to transport coal on the steep trail was not worthwhile. His next grand idea was equally ill-conceived. He commissioned a large, 92-foot steamboat to be built in San Francisco, dismantled, and delivered to Lees Ferry where it was re-assembled. The ship was intended to carry enough coal to enable the gold sluicing operation to finally be successful, or at least under a full head of steam. Alas, the large, coal-fired ship needed to consume most of the coal it transported in order to power its own boilers. The entire operation was shut down in 1912. The *Charles H. Spencer* was de-commissioned and ultimately sunk in several feet of water where it is still visible just below the surface of the river from the riverside trail. Spencer's ill-conceived operation lasted about a year and was abandoned in 1912.[6]

While you're in the Vermilion Cliffs and Marble Canyon areas, there are many other interesting things to see and do. Here's a brief list of some of the other attractions and agencies:

Antelope Canyon Tours (several tour vendors located in Page.)

Horseshoe Bend, Page AZ
(1.5 mile round-trip hike to a magnificent overlook)

Jacob's Lake Inn and Restaurant (928) 643-7232

Kaibab Plateau Visitor Center (928) 643-7298

Navajo Bridge Interpretive Center (928) 355-2319

North Kaibab Ranger District (928) 643-7395

North Rim Back-Country Office (928) 638-7868

Vermilion Cliffs Day Tours, Kanab, UT (928) 691-0166

Wire Pass to Buckskin Gulch hike (3.5 miles round-trip). Call (435) 688-3200 for directions.

1. *New York Times*, August 14, 1997.
2. United States Department of the Interior. Title 36, Code of Federal Regulations, Section 2.62(b).
3. Excerpt from www.nps.gov/gcra/planyourvisit/upload.South_Canyon.
4. Vasey's Paradise historic and fauna data from www.azheritagewaters.nau.edu/loc_Vasey'sParadise.html.
5. Stanton's Cave information from www.photographic-exploration.com/bat.html.
6. Charles Spencer information from cpluhna.nau.edu.

John Rominek & Dave Elston at Grapevine Camp.

CHAPTER EIGHT

Clear Creek, Cheyava Falls, and Discovery of Possible Human Remains

You may encounter many defeats, but you must not be defeated. In fact, it may be necessary to encounter the defeats so you can know who you are, what you can rise from, and how you can still come out of it.
Maya Angelou

One of the really great things about the Grand Canyon is that it doesn't take a whole lot of effort to find someplace where it's quiet and you can get away from the crowds. When I am at Phantom Ranch, whether camping or in the dormitories or cabins, one of my favorite day hikes is the trail to Clear Creek. If I'm staying in the lodging, I sign up for the early breakfast, grab a sack lunch as I leave the canteen, and hit the trail for a full day of great hiking, beautiful scenery, and all the solitude I'm looking for. Don't get me wrong, though. I always enjoy the company of good friends since there's so much to share along the trail. Helping family and friends experience magical places in my life is a true joy.

The trail to Clear Creek is not particularly difficult, and walking even part of it during a rest day at Phantom is highly encouraged. The full-length trail is 9.2 miles each way to the Clear Creek campground. However, there are many places to stop along the route, which make great turnarounds, so that you can be back to the Ranch in time for whichever dinner you signed up for.

The trail begins about a quarter-mile north of Phantom Ranch. Simply walk upstream past the laundry area and helipad, and you will soon see a small sign indicating Clear Creek to the right. The trail quickly begins a steep ascent that might make you question your decision, or even my recommendation, to do this hike. However, a few minutes of uphill effort bring hikers to a broad overlook of the entire Phantom Ranch complex. You will have gained about 500 feet in elevation and already distanced yourself from the many hikers and mule riders. The trail again continues an uphill path, and the sweeping views open up further and keep getting get better and better. Once on top of the Tonto Plateau, the trail skirts some large outcroppings to the left and eventually makes a turn toward the east. This is a great destination or turnaround point with fantastic views of the South Rim, the two bridges at the river, and the final set of switchbacks on the South Kaibab Trail. Depending on the time of year, you might not even see anyone else on this section of the trail. Take time to enjoy both the view and the natural quiet.

During a cold, early spring hike to West Clear Creek, I reached this point and thought I could hear music. I looked around a bit and found the unlikely and unforgettable source. A few hundred feet off the trail, and in the middle of the Tonto Plateau, was a small dome tent with a young woman sitting cross-legged on a large, flat rock. She was playing a beautiful silver flute, and her music seemed to enhance the peacefulness of the canyon. How is it possible that so much sound and emotion can come from such a small instrument? I briefly introduced myself and found out she was a seasonal Smoke Jumper from Northern Arizona. She explained that her job was to jump out of airplanes with her firefighting gear on and parachute into "hot zones" that ground-based vehicles couldn't reach. During the rest of the year, when she wasn't risking her life fighting fires, she hiked. I was both impressed and humbled, and I conveniently forgot to tell her that I mostly sit at a desk and occasionally make business trips in airplanes that I don't ever need to jump out of. She wouldn't have been nearly as impressed as I was with her occupation.

If you decide to continue hiking toward Clear Creek, you are in for more treats and some exceptional scenery. Zoroaster Temple is my favorite landmark on this hike, and it will watch over you for most of the remainder of your hike. Zoroaster and its nearby cousin, Sumner Butte, are part of a very large drainage area that funnels occasional rains directly across the trail. When hard rains occur, the resulting flash floods have incised a narrow slot canyon into the Tapeats sandstone as the runoff pushes and shoves everything in its way toward the Colorado River. This easily identified drainage is Sumner Wash and is located 6.7 miles from Phantom Ranch.

It was during this early spring hike that I decided to stop in the middle of the slickrock trail where it crosses Sumner Wash and enjoy my lunch. While I ate, I studied the section of the wash that was well upstream of the trail and noticed a shallow cave approximately 12'-15' above the wide streambed. It was on the west side of the wash, and would have made an excellent afternoon shady spot for the indigenous people who lived in the canyon.

I decided to investigate. Since there were no other hikers around, I left my backpack and water bottle in the middle of the trail and made my way a few hundred yards up the wash bed. Several paces before the cave I discovered a small, rectangular stone wall about waist high, and it appeared to have been divided into two rooms. Now I was confident I was on to something. I began to climb the scree slope directly beneath the shallow cave and spotted an arrowhead, then a second, a third, and even a fourth in the brief seconds it took to reach the cave. There were also numerous flakes and pieces of pottery scattered everywhere. When I pushed myself up and onto the ledge, I came face-to-face with what appeared to be a human skeleton. The skull and left leg were missing and the remains were "chest up." By my rough estimate, the skeleton would have been about 4.5 feet tall. No clothing was anywhere in the dry overhang and a few bones and several well-worn teeth were scattered around the floor. I very gently touched a lower rib bone, and it easily broke off. The skeleton had been there for a very long time, and the bones appeared to have been disturbed by scavengers.

I was both humbled and jolted as I returned to my backpack. I didn't have an appetite for the rest of my lunch so I donned my pack and continued the remaining 2.5 miles to Clear Creek. I recall thinking about how easy our lives are today when compared to what our ancestors had to deal with. I also recall wondering what to do about the skeleton I'd found. Should I report it, should I bury it, or should I just try to forget about it? No chance of the latter!

Clear Creek campground was cold and damp. There were two other small groups at the campground, but I found a small spot to place my tent near the creek. The sun was nearly gone by the time I had made camp, and I quickly pumped and filtered some creek water and set it on my trusty MSR stove to come to a boil. A good dehydrated meal (a relative term), hot herbal tea with honey, and a few cookies put me in a better mood and I quickly fell asleep. Tomorrow I would wander upstream in search of the always elusive and ephemeral Cheyava Falls and then make the hike back to Phantom Ranch.

Cheyava Falls is an enigma. It's the tallest waterfall in Arizona but disappears for most of the year. If winter or spring provides sufficient snow or rain, the falls comes alive and tumbles 800 feet down the Redwall limestone into Clear Creek.[1] When there hasn't been much moisture, the falls is more a small trickle issuing from an aquifer about 400 feet from the top.

The falls went unnoticed for a long time. In 1903 a prospector reported he had seen a very large sheet of ice at the headwaters of Clear Creek. In 1908, after Dave Rust had installed a passenger cable across the Colorado River, the energetic and determined Kolb brothers set out to investigate. After their trans-canyon hike, and a difficult ascent with large cameras and photographic plates, they reported that the suspected sheet of ice was actually a very large waterfall. They subsequently named it "Cheyava," which is a Hopi word for intermittent waters.[2] The famous brothers resorted to heroic measures to obtain the first photographs of the falls, and a tour of their studio at the South Rim offers many other dramatic early photos of the Canyon area.

Intrigued and spurred on by their difficult and historic visit, Emery and Ellsworth made several return trips to the falls. They also made a daring and unprecedented exploration of the water-carved cave from which the falls emanates. Here is an excerpt from their notes:

> *The cave as described by my brother is approximately 60 feet high at the entrance, with the lower opening blocked by huge rocks which have fallen from the ceiling. Inside, the ceiling extends upward in the shape of a dome,*

100 to 150 feet in height. The width is about 100 feet and a lake extends about 600 feet back. This is divided by a huge rock or ledge necessitating the use of a 20-foot ladder. There are no stalactites of importance but many lime crystals and incrustations are in evidence.[3]

My exploration of Cheyava Falls was not as successful or memorable as the Kolb brother's was. I woke before sunrise and began boiling water for tea and instant oatmeal. While the water heated, I forced my tent and sleeping bag into their stuff sacks, deflated my sleeping pad, and warmed my hands over the small, white gas flames. I readied my daypack with water, a small can of chicken salad, and what turned out to be some really bad tortillas. For the record, tortillas made from spelt flour sound like a good idea, and are probably really good for you, but don't expect them to remain in one piece on a lengthy backpacking trip. As the Bible says, "For you were made from dust, and to dust you will return," (Genesis 3:19) so do spelt flour tortillas! They had degenerated into a pile of crumbs at the bottom of the Ziploc bag.

I began hiking upstream, being careful not to awaken the other groups still sleeping. My progress seemed slow as I gradually gained altitude and, on occasion, had to work my way through seemingly endless tall grasses and cat claw. I eventually arrived at Obi Canyon and some ancient ruins, and was soon confused which direction to head from here. There were two canyons intersecting Clear Creek, and I had forgotten my topo map in my backpack at camp. As bad luck would have it, I selected the wrong canyon and ended up in a beautiful area full of cottonwood trees-but no waterfall. I ate my lunch, such that it was, and decided to return to camp, collect my backpack, and make the 9.2-mile return hike to Phantom Ranch. Although my attempt to visit Cheyava Falls was a bust, it was still a great hike. Sometimes the journey proves more worthwhile than the destination.

When I returned to my creek side campsite, there was no one around. There were only three or four recognizable campsites in those days, and they were vacant in expectation of new arrivals. It was around noon, and I assumed the people I'd met the previous evening in camp were on their way somewhere else. As I made the long slog up the slippery, peach-colored Hakatai Shale, I saw a group of four hikers ahead of me. I caught up to them when they took a rest break and learned they had visited Cheyava Falls yesterday. They had been disappointed with the small amount of flow, but it secretly made me happy knowing I hadn't spent a lot of time locating the falls, just to be disillusioned, as well. I told them I had been "temporarily misplaced" earlier in the day, which brought a little humor to our sweaty group. They were heading to Bright Angel campground at Phantom Ranch for two nights, and I was really looking forward to my dormitory bed, a hot shower, a stew dinner, and no more spelt tortillas if I arrived in time.

Our group passed Sumner Wash by mid-afternoon, and I made no mention of the skeleton I'd found the day before. During my fitful sleep the previous night, I had made the decision to report my find at Phantom Ranch and let them do their thing. But, what if the skeleton turned out to not be human? What if it was simply an animal with similar bone structure? Given the context of an ancient stone wall, man-made arrowheads and pottery shards and stone flakes scattered everywhere, I felt it was an appropriate assumption.

With only about three miles to go, I said good-bye to the group and increased my pace in order to get back to Phantom Ranch before the 6:30pm dinner bell. I told my new hiking friends I would be in the canteen later in the evening when it re-opened at 8:00 pm for snacks and camaraderie.

After a very early breakfast, I was packed and ready to hike out via the South Kaibab Trail. Since I was hiking alone, I was going to try to beat my personal record of 2 hours and 57 minutes from the canteen steps to the top of the rim. Not a spectacular effort, but a pace of approximately 2.5 mile per hour. The South Kaibab Trail is fully exposed to the sun, so it's not the right choice of trails in the hotter months. Add the fact that it's steep and has no water, and most people elect to take a combination of the River and Bright Angel trails from Phantom Ranch to the South Rim.

Just as I was getting ready to depart from the dormitory steps, a park ranger walked past me on his way to the canteen. I stopped him and described the skeleton I'd found. We went inside the canteen to the large topo map displayed on the wall. I did my best to describe exactly where to find the remains, and he took several notes as well as my name, e-mail and office phone number. Those were the days before cell phones.

My solo hike up the South Kaibab went well, but I didn't set a new personal record. I don't typically keep track of such things anyway, but I had once been part of a group of 10 people in a cabin at Phantom Ranch, and nine of them were engineers from Intel. Each of us had been requested to bring a bottle of liquor from a different country. I recall that I brought Tia Maria from Mexico. At some point during our last night, and as part of an engineering-type drinking game, someone had the brainy idea to keep track of how long it took each of us to hike out. I was the second person out and somehow never forgot my time.

And, if you're wondering, I didn't hear anything from the Park Service about the skeleton I had found. However, I wouldn't rest until the skeleton had been put to rest as well.

1. Information from hikearizona.com/decoder.php?ZTN=15318.
2. Information from nps.gov/gcra/planyourvisit/upload/Clear_Creek_Trail.pdf.
3. Grand Canyon Historical Society, *The Ol' Pioneer*, Jul/Aug/Sep 2004; Volume 15, Number 3.

Dave Rust's cable car across the Colorado River. Courtesy of NPS.

*View of Zoroaster from the overhang in Sumner Wash.
Courtesy of Jim McCarthy.*

CHAPTER NINE

Sumner Wash Revisited

When man is away from Nature his heart becomes hard.
Native American proverb

Over the next several years, as our daughter and son became involved in high school activities and established their identities and independence, I found myself able to get away for more frequent backpacking trips. I had logged about 275 days in the Grand Canyon and was thinking that I should set a personal goal of 365 days—*a year in one of the best places on earth!* A park ranger at the Visitor's Center told me that there were likely less than fifty civilians or non-Park Service employees alive today who had seen and hiked as much of the Grand Canyon as I had. I joined a couple of online backpacking groups, and I quickly became aware of many intriguing routes, loop hikes, aggressive day hikes, and even a few obscure side canyons awaiting my exploration. Our family also took a six-day commercial river trip from Lee's Ferry to Diamond Creek. It was fantastic to have access, albeit for only short afternoons or excursions before dinner or breakfast, to so many places I had heard and read about but had never explored.

As my relationships grew with some of the members of my new hiking clubs and on-line communities, I was intrigued and amazed to learn about the countless issues related to managing a fragile and complex resource the size of Grand Canyon. Some of the major issues included helicopter tour operations vs. the concept of "Natural Quiet"; the federally-mandated mix of commercial vs. private boaters; uranium exploration and mining near the South Rim; and the never-ending intentions of developers hoping to capitalize on the millions of tourists visiting the Grand Canyon each year. I have developed a deep and genuine respect for the many people who love the Canyon as I do, and who make the necessary sacrifices and commitments to act as stewards and protectors of the fragile place we all love.

In late March 2004, my good friend, Jim and I received a five-day permit to hike from the South Rim to Clear Creek. This would be my first opportunity to revisit "The Bones" at Sumner Wash. Jim had recently completed his Master's thesis on the concept of natural quiet within the Grand Canyon, and he took the opportunity of a multi-day trip to define the concept to me:

> *Natural Quiet is not necessarily silence: It includes natural sounds such as wind through the pines, the cascading call of the canyon wren, the subtle sound of slow flowing streams, the roar of rapids and waterfalls, and myriad other bold and delicate sounds.*[1]

As we made our way toward our lunch destination at Sumner Wash, I told Jim we'd be checking to see if the bones I had found were still there. We spent a couple of hours exploring the narrow Tapeats Sandstone slot canyon below the trail, ate our sack lunch from Phantom Ranch, and then hiked up the wide wash toward the overhang that had held me in suspense for the past several years.

The bones were awaiting my return. They had, however, been further disturbed and scattered since my initial discovery. I found a tooth in the soft sand, a molar that had been ground nearly flat. Native Americans foraged and grew seeds and grains, which they ground into flour with stone metatas and manos (similar to a mortar and pestle). Finely crushed stone is a by-product of this process, and it would mix with the flour and cause rapid and extensive wearing of teeth. Jim had brought a large-format camera with him on our day hike. He sat down near the bones and took an impressive photo of the view of Zoroaster.

After our hike, we contacted park officials to report the suspected human bones. We must have found the right person. Several months later, Jim received a call that the NPS was interested in viewing the bones and assuring a proper burial. Plans were made for a representative from the NPS to hike with Jim and me on a three-night, round-trip hike to Sumner Wash. As the hike date approached, I needed to go on a business trip. Jim was still available, and he remembered where the overhang was located.

On November 15, 2004, Jim and Ellen Brennan, a NPS Vanishing Treasures representative, began their hike toward Sumner Wash. After a night at Bright Angel Campground, they reached their destination the next day. Ms. Brennan was not 100% sure the bones were human, but she took every precaution to treat them with utmost respect and care. As she dug a shallow grave, she unearthed a 5" stone scraper that had been hand-hewn by a Native American artisan. It was knapped to a sharp edge on one side and slightly resembled a very large arrowhead. She buried the bones and scraper in the shallow grave and took a photo.

In a region as large as the Grand Canyon, caves and shallow overhangs such as the one I discovered are commonplace. According to the National Park Service:

> *Hidden within the Grand Canyon are an estimated 1,000 caves. Of those, 335 have been recorded. Very few have been mapped or inventoried. Most have developed in the limestone of the Redwall and Muav formations, although some are known to exist in other formations.*[2]

I asked Michael Ghiglieri, co-author of *Over the Edge: Death in Grand Canyon*, whether discovery of human, or presumed human, remains in the Grand Canyon are tracked and reported in his book. His poignant reply to me was as follows:

> *Regarding your probably Native American skeleton, it is always interesting and eerie to come upon these recondite archaeology sites in the Canyon (or anywhere for that matter) and find human remains. It is sobering, humbling, and spurs the imagination into high gear trying to guess what sad event led to the death of the person found. But, as with your find, we cannot use it in Over the Edge because no real evidence exists as to the manner in which the victim died. Thus there is really no information beyond the interesting reality that the desert climate and dearth of bone gnawing rodents in these overhangs or caves has allowed the survival of desiccated bones for centuries. In*

short, there are lots of Native America [sic] slowly crumbling to dust in the Canyon, but very few allow the forensics needed to reconstruct their manner of death.

My goal of a respectful interment of the presumed human bones had been accomplished. The Park Service was quick to react, accommodating with their approach, and respectful in their duties. I couldn't have anticipated a better response, and am grateful to my long-time friend, Jim, for helping me finally close this unresolved issue in my Grand Canyon adventures.

1. Additional information on Natural Quiet in the Grand Canyon can be found in The National Parks Overflights Act of 1987, Section 3.

2. arizonageology.blogspot.com

CHAPTER TEN

Fun on the Colorado River

> *Life should not be a journey to the grave with the intention of arriving safely in a pretty and well preserved body, but rather to skid in broadside in a cloud of smoke, thoroughly used up, totally worn out, and loudly proclaiming "Wow! What a Ride!"*
> Hunter S. Thompson

You hear it before you see it. The nearly silent rumble is masked by the conversation on the boat, but it's definitely there. Soon, you feel a slight vibration and rumble in your chest. You stand up in the boat, look anxiously downstream, and notice a lick of frothy water shoot up from below the river horizon, and just as quickly disappear. If you are not paying attention to the delicate and subtle sounds of the Canyon, you might never know what's about to happen until it's too late to prepare. Almost imperceptibly, your boat begins to pick up speed as it's pulled into the smooth, silent tongue and strong wave trains of the approaching rapid. You grab onto the rope hand lines and cautiously think to yourself, "*This will be a good one!*" Suddenly, someone shouts "*Suck rubber!*"

They come in all shapes, sizes, and intensities. They have all manner of personalities, legend, lore, and mishaps behind their names. Badger, Soap, House Rock, Tanner, Hance, Sockdolager, Grapevine, Horn, Hermit, Sapphire, Crystal, Upset, and Lava. These are only a few personal favorites of the more than 150 named rapids in the Grand Canyon. And they sure do draw a crowd!

The River

The once wild and seasonal Colorado River, impounded since 1966 behind massive Glen Canyon Dam, is born from rains and snowmelt in the 14,000' Rocky Mountains near Grand Lake, Colorado. It is joined by the Green River in southeastern Utah and flows into Lake Powell, the second largest, but slowly dwindling, man-made lake in the United States. As it comes to rest in the lake, it unloads its massive load of silt and debris, the equivalent of 1,400 ship cargo containers each day.[1] At the other end of the 180-mile-long lake, the river slowly discharges from the bottom of the 710' high dam at about 4 miles per hour. The river has been dramatically altered. It is no longer warm and flaccid in the summer, nor cold and wild in the winter and spring. It has lost its spirit. It has been impounded, and it has been temporarily tamed. The river now runs clear and consistently cold, about 47°, and it rises and falls like the tides of the oceans. The slow, irregular heartbeat of these constant fluctuations is not driven by gravitational pull and moon phases. Rather, it is caused by the pervasive electrical demands of arid desert cities like Las Vegas and Phoenix. River levels rise and fall as the very cold water at the bottom of the dam is forced through massive spinning turbines. These turbines generate hydroelectricity to keep us cool in the summer and warm in the winter. Will you be running the rapids on a weekend when air-conditioned office buildings, banks, and schools are mostly empty and don't need to be cooled? Be prepared for lower river levels, and the challenges and consequences of guiding your brightly painted wooden or inflated boat over the gnarly boulders and bedrock lurking just below the surface of the low, constantly changing water.

Does this sound like fun? Are you up for an adventure of a lifetime? A rafting trip through the Grand Canyon is a "bucket list" item for many people. My wife and I have been on several commercial, and one private river trip, and would drop everything to go again if we ever have the opportunity. Therein lies the rub! Demand far exceeds the regulated passenger capacity of the river. In October 2003, we were fortunate to join a private river trip. My close friend and permit holder was overjoyed. He had waited more than a decade for his name to be drawn!

I would be remiss if I didn't dedicate at least one chapter in this book to rafting the Colorado River through the Grand Canyon. Hundreds of excellent books have been written about the river's colorful history, the numerous environmental and litigious challenges facing it today, how to safely run the rapids, where to explore after you make camp, etc. In keeping with the theme of this book, I will introduce readers to some interesting history and geology, recall some favorite experiences, and make a few recommendations for how to get the most out of a river trip. If it's on *your* bucket list, I hope you can go. You won't regret it!

Rafting Choices

There are two types of river trips-commercial and private. Commercial concessioners are awarded the majority of available passenger slots, while private boaters typically wait years and years for their permit to be awarded. Regulations are quite complicated and subject to occasional change, so it's advisable to check for the latest updated information.

A commercial trip is a "for profit" trip hosted by a commercial river running company. Trip duration is from 3 to 18 days, and the waiting list is typically 1-2 years. Currently, there are 16 NPS-approved concessioners. This list can be accessed at www.nps.gov/gcra/river-concessioners.htm.

Private trips, as the name implies, are rowing trips organized and led by private individuals possessing the requisite experience and supplies to assure a safe trip. Private trips must be "non-profit," and passengers are only allowed one trip per year. Since private trips are usually non-motorized, and river progress is slower with more freedom to explore the canyon, trip duration is from 12 to 25 days. The waiting period to receive a permit under the new weighted lottery system is usually extensive. Information and regulations can be accessed at www.nps.gov/overview-lees-ferry-diamond.htm.

Private and commercial trips all launch from Lee's Ferry-River at River Mile Zero. Passengers often spend their last night of "civilization" at Marble Canyon Lodge before their launch in the morning. However, once you have done a river trip, you might come to think that true civilization begins at Lee's Ferry rather than ends there. Marble Canyon Lodge is only a few short miles from Lee's Ferry and they have a good restaurant and nice rooms. There are also two other lodges to stay at in the general area, Cliff Dwellers Lodge and Lee's Ferry Lodge. They both have good restaurants and nice rooms, and are a few minutes further up Highway 89A from Lee's Ferry.

On the day before a commercial trip, and if you have the time, I recommend you drive to Lee's Ferry in the late afternoon or early evening before sunset. You will likely have an opportunity to meet your crew, and perhaps other passengers from your upcoming trip, as well. Be sure to stick your toes in the cold Colorado River for good luck. If you have more time, drive back to Highway 89A and visit the Old Navajo Bridge and excellent interpretive center. Look 467 feet down to the placid Colorado River. Where are the rapids? It seems like a very peaceful and calm river from the bridge. However, you will find out its true character tomorrow after you pass under it in the first few river miles of your trip. Before you leave the bridge, spend some time looking for California condors that sometimes pass this way between Grand Canyon and Lake Powell.

A Typical Day on a Commercial River Trip

After a good dinner and a restful final night in a cozy bed, you will wake up early, grab some breakfast, and meet your ride to Lee's Ferry. If you have a vehicle, move it to the small, dirt parking area across the street from the lodge, and leave your car keys with the front desk. Make that last cell phone call, send that last text or Facebook update, and be sure to write down your passwords. You're "Goin' In" for a while!

When you arrive at Lee's Ferry in the morning, it will be buzzing with activity. There are usually a mix of private and commercial boats launching each day, and the level of excitement and anticipation is always high. You won't believe the amount of cargo these boats can carry and still remain well above water. The massive amount of beer, wine, and soda they can hold is always impressive to me, and I do my best to lighten the load as the trip progresses.

Your participation, and your adrenaline levels, will begin to increase when the crew asks you to pick out a life jacket (a Personal Flotation Device, or PFD). Make sure it fits you well and is not too big or too small. The PFD is your new best friend and partner, and you will wear it proudly the entire time you are in the boat. Soon after, you will form a fire brigade line, and assist in loading the duffel bags and beverages each of you have brought. After all the gear is stowed, and the crew has completed their checklist and final discussions with the local park ranger, you will receive a safety briefing from your crew. Now, it's time to get your new river shoes wet. Step into the boat, find a suitable spot, grab your camera, and start what most people agree is the best adventure they have ever had! You are about to become a River Rat!

Within a few minutes of calmly drifting away from Lee's Ferry, you will encounter the Paria Riffle. It's a small wrinkle in an otherwise smooth river, but it will be the first action you will experience. Your fellow passengers will cool down as their new river clothes experience the first splashes of the cold Colorado River.

Most of the river is actually smooth water. The majority of the 150+ rapids you will encounter were caused by occasional flash flooding of side canyons that flow into the main river. Extensive and powerful rains will occasionally flood the side canyons and force large rocks, sometimes the size of automobiles, into the river channel. At lower river flows, these submerged and typically invisible debris fans can become dangerously exposed. If a side canyon has recently flashed, river guides will often pull ashore in advance and study the changed rapids for a new "line."

On August 9, 2015, brief but heavy rains in the House Rock Valley and Vermilion Cliffs areas caused extensive flooding and impressive road damage. This remote and rocky region received 1.5" of afternoon rain in less than 20 minutes. Dozens of large, 15' diameter boulders, many of which needed to be dynamited before road crews could move them, were carried 2 miles from the cliffs and came to rest on what was left of Highway 89A. The attention of the state-wide news reports was on the unforeseen road closure, as it should have been. However, a small section of the eastern Grand Canyon felt the effects, too. The flood waters that removed the road and damaged the bridge gathered speed, volume, and debris load as the gradient increased just past the roadway. The raging waters raced downhill into the many narrow side canyons and tributaries that join together and flow into the Soap Creek drainage. When the massive debris of boulders, sand, trees and shrubbery was injected directly into Soap Creek Rapids, the river quickly turned from blue-green to a reddish-brown. Soap Creek Rapids immediately moved up in difficulty, climbing from a moderate rating of 5 to an adventurous rating of 7. For several weeks after the flood, river guides were cautioned to pull off the river and "read" the changed rapids before attempting what used to be a straightforward run down the middle. The boulders have now settled in on the river floor and it no longer seems so different.

Even though the Colorado River is known for its extensive rapids, the calmer sections of the river are equally impressive. Commercial motorized trips use relatively quiet, four-stroke motors to propel and steer their large, inflatable boats. Although the motors are certainly noisier than a boat with no motor, passengers get used to it on a weeklong trip. A coalition of commercial river companies is currently working to develop a hybrid-electric motor as an eventual replacement for the 30-horsepower, gasoline motors used today. The Colorado River needs all the help it can get. According to Western Rivers, an environmental conservancy and advocacy group, it is the most endangered river in the nation.

Quiet times on the river are meant for observing, conversing, and learning more about nature, geology, history, and yourself. During one memorable trip, near river mile 30, we noticed a peregrine falcon, once known as a "duck hawk," pursuing a young duckling floating by itself on the river. Our guide shut off the motor, and we silently drifted and watched the duckling. Each time the falcon would fly up behind the duckling and try to pluck it from the water, the duckling would quickly dive under the water and avoid capture. This process repeated itself at least a dozen times. When the duckling floated near a sand bar in the middle of the river, he quickly waddled ashore and hid under the small reeds. Not easily outsmarted, the falcon landed on the sand bar and pursued the duckling once again. It was not a fair fight. We were treated to a small, but poignant example of a daily life-and-death struggle as we comfortably drifted through the soaring, red walls of the Canyon.

During a quiet time on the river, your guide will probably explain the Desert Rivers Rapid Classification Scale used in the Grand Canyon. It's a quick method to identify the severity of the many rapids. Most rapids have two numerical ratings–one for high flows and one for low flows. Surprisingly, most rapids are more dangerous at low flows, but some can be more dangerous at high flows. The Grand Canyon rapids scale is a unique, ten-point rating system. All other rivers and waterways in the U.S. are rated on a six-point system known as the International Scale of River Difficulty. You will certainly impress your friends if you know the difference between the two scales.

Once you've been through Paria Riffle, Badger Creek Rapids, and possibly Soap Creek Rapids, it should be time for lunch and a well-deserved bio break. This is where newly-minted River Rats begin learning more new and exciting things. If you are on a private trip, you will locate a cooler labeled Day 1, or some similar nomenclature, and you will set about preparing your first lunch on the river. If you are on a commercial trip, lunch will be made for you while you stretch your newly acquired sea legs. Rafting and camping in the Grand Canyon are done on a "zero impact" basis. This means that everything, including all litter, food scraps and crumbs, and fecal waste, are removed. There should be no trace, other than footprints, that you have been there.

Now, about that well-deserved bio break. The guides will tell you that the official bathroom is set up after you locate a suitable beach and make camp for the evening. Meanwhile, as the need arises you simply pee in the river. Admittedly, men have it much easier in this regard. Men must pee directly into the river and not on the sand. This usually necessitates standing at least ankle deep in the cold water. However, in order for women to pee into the river they must wade into the water waist-deep, fully clothed…or not! The extremely cold water, not to mention the embarrassment of everyone else knowing exactly what you are doing, is no cause for alarm. Most women tend to "group up" and find a discreet location to wade into the water. By the end of your river trip, no one will think twice about the process, and embarrassment will be a distant memory.

As exciting as running wild rapids is, one of the other great things about a river trip is the many side hikes and explorations you have access to. Your guides will be familiar with the best beaches to stop at for lunch and evening camps, as well as the sights to see and explore once you are off the boat and are anxious to do some exploring. Hiking and exploring is certainly not a required activity. If you have physical limitations, or would rather read a book or write in your journal, this is your trip to enjoy and experience as you please.

Without a doubt, the most memorable river excursion I ever had occurred when we stopped at Blacktail Canyon (river mile 120.9) for lunch. Our guides recommended we take an hour or so to hike into the narrow slot canyon while they prepared lunch. My wife and my 75 and 76-year-old parents were with me as we walked the short, flat path into the very narrow and darkening canyon. We marveled at the brown walls, which were several hundred feet high and nearly blocked our narrow views of the sky. At some point during our walk, my father asked if we could hear music. We stopped, listened, and indeed could hear faint classical music. The volume increased as we continued our walk. As we rounded a final bend and reached the end of the canyon, we were shocked beyond words. There, sitting on bailing buckets and boat cushions, were four people playing musical instruments. A cello, two violins, and a viola made up the unlikely ensemble. As the rest of our group eventually filled the small chamber, the music briefly stopped. We learned that the ensemble were all members of the Montreal Symphony in Canada. They brought their delicate instruments to entertain themselves, and anyone else lucky enough to be in the area. They went on to play a wonderful piece of hauntingly beautiful classical music, and there wasn't a dry eye in the audience. With a trickling waterfall at the back of the canyon, and best friends and family with me in my favorite place, I couldn't imagine anywhere else I'd rather be.

Afternoons on the river are always great times. When the water is placid and the sun is warm, large squirt guns often come out of hiding, cold beers and sodas are pulled from the drag bags, and life on the river gets really good. Wildlife is abundant in the Canyon, and they make their way to the cool water to drink and enjoy the shade and camouflage of the tamarisk and redbud trees.

In fact, there are more than 90 species of mammals in the Grand Canyon—even more than in Yellowstone National Park.[2] Of the 90+ species, 34 are found along the Colorado River today. A few favorites of mine are beaver, bats, ringtails, bighorn sheep, mule deer, and birds of all sizes and sounds. Desert bighorn sheep are well suited to the rocky slopes and cliffs they live and play on. It's a real treat to see a small band of them putting on a display of their gravity-defying abilities when they realize that boats are approaching. They will see you long before you see them.

By mid-afternoon, your guide will begin looking for a suitable beach to establish camp for the evening. Guides often have favorite beaches in mind, but they cannot be reserved in advance. Group size, and pace of the trip, typically plays into the decision where to camp.

Grand Canyon beaches are usually several feet above river level, and are located on "river right" or river left." After a picket has been driven into the sand, and a rope or two has been secured to a rock or tree, it is time to unload the boat. The outhouse, or "Groover," is usually one of the first things to be set up and the last to be taken down the following morning. Everyone assists with unloading of the waterproof dry bags with your belongings in them. Stick around to help with unloading the tents, sleeping bags, cots, propane tanks, stoves, shade screens, camp chairs, dish and hand washing kits, and possibly the fire pans. You might see one of your guides place a vertical stick of driftwood into the sand at the exact point where the beach and the river meet. This is a non-scientific, but accurate river gauge. Over time, it will tell observers whether the river's tide is rising or falling.

Once the boat is unloaded, you can set about finding a suitable area on the beach to pitch your tent. I typically sleep on a cot under the stars rather than pitch a tent, but will use one if there is a chance of rain or blowing dust, or both. On commercial trips, the crew will start food preparation while the passengers begin exploring the area, updating journals, or gathering in groups in anticipation of Happy Hour breaking out. If you decide to explore, be sure to take some water, tell a guide where you are going and how long you intend to be gone, and bring someone else with you. The guides can help you decide what to safely see and do.

Evening on the river is truly a great time. It's an opportunity to recall and revisit the events of the day with all the members of your party—not just those that were on your particular boat. It's a chance to learn about your guides and your fellow passengers. There is usually more than enough food, and sometimes a surprise dessert will appear from the cooler or a hot Dutch oven. After dishes are washed and put away, guitars, recorders, flutes, and harmonicas often make an appearance. Just imagine enjoying a great dinner while you are several thousand feet below the canyon rims, cut-off from everything but yourself, your friends, and your family. Then imagine hearing the steady call of the rapids you will experience the first thing tomorrow morning. Imagine the moon rising over the massive but silent canyon walls, bats hunting and diving in the fading daylight, the descending crescendo of the canyon wren, and singing along with the music of your friends, and of the canyon. Life is good, and it's even better on the river!

Evening discussions often focus on what you saw and did today, and what's on the agenda for tomorrow. If luck is with you, a guide or passenger will bring up the legendary story of Glen and Bessie Hyde, the "Honeymoon Couple." Their intriguing and unresolved mystery, now nearly 90 years old, still fascinates river runners and Grand Canyon historians, and makes a great campfire story.

The wild, early days of river exploration in the Grand Canyon were filled with an assortment of colorful characters, trials and errors, deadly mishaps, and occasional but infrequent success. By 1928, it had been 59 years since John Wesley Powell's historic exploration of the entire Grand Canyon by boat. As testament to the difficulty of the trip, only 45 men had successfully followed in Powell's historic footsteps by then.

Newlyweds, Glen and Bessie Hyde, hatched a plan to build a crude boat, a sweep scow, and float through the Grand Canyon. When successful, Bessie would become the first woman to complete the trip, and they were certain that fame, fortune, and endless speaking engagements and public interest would quickly follow. Glen had dabbled with canoes and other small boats when he lived in the Pacific Northwest for a few years, and he had also piloted a scow in Idaho. Bessie was petite and attractive, and intended to keep a detailed journal of their adventure. She anxiously supported her newest husband's plan to raft for a couple of months, and then become eternally famous as the first woman to complete a river trip through the Grand Canyon.

They launched their newly constructed scow, *Rain in the Face*, on the placid Green River, and enjoyed smooth sailing all the way to the confluence with the Colorado River. They survived several close calls in Cataract Canyon, but eventually emerged at Lee's Ferry to begin their soon-to-be-famous trip through the Grand Canyon. Along the way, they visited newly constructed Phantom Ranch, and also hiked up the Bright Angel Trail for a lunch meeting with Emery Kolb and his family. They had already survived many harrowing and close calls, and were running low on supplies. Bessie seemed dejected and confided to Emery's wife, Blanche, that she was unsure she would ever come out of the canyon. Emery tried to convince Glen to take life preservers, but his experienced pleas fell on proud and deaf ears.

Once back on the river, Glen and Bessie somehow ran several more increasingly treacherous and demoralizing rapids. Battered and wet in the cold November weather, they eventually arrived at Hermit Creek Camp where their new supplies were waiting. Spectators noted that Bessie was agitated, nervous, and demanding to leave the river. It was not to be. Glen forced her back into the scow and they departed, once again, toward their presumed destiny of fame and fortune. Remarkably, but not without extreme difficulties, they survived Crystal and Lava Rapids, among many others.

Bessie's journal noted their passing of Diamond Creek (river mile 229.1) and also their running of 231 Mile Rapid, but her journal suddenly ended at this point. It was November 30, 1928. They had marked 42 days of progress in their boat, and had traveled 232.5 miles on the unforgiving and largely unexplored river of the Grand Canyon.

Their adventure had ended, but how did it end, and were they alive or dead?

Bessie loved to write poetry, and she had once penned a poem, titled *Mermaid Doll*:

> *Oh! Mama dear, please come*
> *My dolly must be drowned,*
> *When I put her in the creek,*
> *She sunk without a sound.*
> *Wee Betty's eyes filled with tears,*
> *Where could poor dolly be?*
> *Perhaps she's turned into a mermaid,*
> *And drifted out to sea.*

The newlywed couple never arrived in Needles, California, on December 6 as widely anticipated. Glen's father, Rollin, didn't waste any time setting up search parties and rallying support. Rewards for information were promised, boats full of experienced river runners were dispatched, people were interviewed, and airplanes flew along the river. The abandoned scow was eventually spotted, and the Kolb brothers arrived on the scene in their hastily launched boat on Christmas Eve, 1928.[3]

They found the derelict upright in very quiet water not far from shore and near Gneiss Rapid at 236.5 Mile. Both sweeps were in the water. The bow line was tightly fastened below the water, and they could not release it. In the craft was food, bedding, camera equipment, and clothing, including heavy leather jackets and hiking boots. Glen's gun, a camera with some exposed film, and Bessie's tiny logbook kept in a sort of code were intact. Cut in the gunwale were 42 notches, one for each day. About a foot of water had seeped into the bilge, but no damage was apparent to the hull or sweeps. Salvage included the gun, the Kolb book, a leather jacket, and Bessie's diary.

As with any romantic, unsolved mystery, colorful theories grew out of campfires and ignorance as to the newlywed couple's fate. Could

Glen and Bessy Hyde's Scow, "Rain in the Face," November 1928. Courtesy of National Park Service.

they have been attacked and killed? Did they drown in the river? If so, why were their bodies never recovered? Did they attempt to hike out, and their remains have not yet been found? Was their disappearance part of their plan, only to emerge later to even greater fanfare?

Their bodies were never found, and legends, folklore, and mystery abound to this day. For example, in 1971, an elderly woman on a commercial river trip claimed she was the fabled Bessie Hyde. She admitted that she had stabbed and killed her husband, and that she had successfully hiked out of the canyon. However, she later confessed that she had made up the story.

A captivating and extensively researched account of the Honeymoon Couple's trip can be read in *Sunk Without a Sound: The Tragic Colorado River Honeymoon of Glen and Bessie Hyde*, by Brad Dimock.

With fun mysteries like this to consider, and "Day One" behind you, your mind may wander as you crawl into your sleeping bag for the night. This is what you paid lots of money for, and waited so long for. This is better than you ever imagined it could be. This is your first night on the world famous Colorado River, and you did great. Your stomach is full, and so is your spirit. You'll wish all your friends and loved ones could experience this, too.

Many more rapids lie ahead in the days to come, and most are bigger and wilder than today's were. Many memories and new adventures lie ahead, too. You will walk in a sandy, river-carved cave large enough to hold 5,000 people. You will frolic like a child in the warm, turquoise-blue waters of the Little Colorado River. You will visit an ancient and sacred Native American granary high on a cliff above the river. You may hike to, and be able to touch, one of the oldest fossils on our planet.[4] You will pass by massive lava flows, which have dammed and blocked the path of the Colorado River at least 12 times. You will experience, and maybe jump into, some of the most beautiful and delicate waterfalls in the Grand Canyon. You will soak in the warm, turquoise waters of Havasu Creek and watch as it gently toys with, and then joins, the cold, deep waters of the Colorado River. If your trip has enough time, you might be able to hike up to the wonderful

Running Lava Falls Rapid. Courtesy of National Park Service.

Redwall Cavern with family and friends.

"patio" at Deer Creek, and possibly hike upstream from there to the "throne room" to witness where Deer Creek erupts out of a hidden aquifer in the limestone. You will run, and never forget, famous Crystal Rapids and Lava Rapids, two of the wildest navigable rapids in North America. You will be completely soaked, and probably very cold, and you will love it!

    The scenery, the friendships, the food, and the unencumbered freedom and opportunity to experience it all will get better each day. And, all too soon, your trip will come to an end. You will leave your new river friends and get back to your daily life. You will be glad you wrote your computer passwords down. You will often recall the peaceful and exciting days and nights on the river. Now, you are a River Rat. And, if you are like me, you will still hear the unique and mournful call of the canyon wren wondering if you will ever return.

1. *Orion* magazine, "Calamity on the Colorado," July/August 2010 edition.
2. From http://www.nps.gov/grca/learn/nature/mammals.htm.

3. General information, and direct quotes are from the book, *From Powell to Power*, Otis Reed "Dock" Marston., Vishnu Temple Press, Flagstaff, AZ., 2014.

4. Stromatolites in the Grand Canyon are limestone outcroppings formed by ancient bacteria, and are approximately 740 million to 1.2 billion years old. Data from various sources, including http://www.nps.gov.gcra/learn/nature/fossils.htm.

Deer Creek Falls. Courtesy of NPS.

CHAPTER ELEVEN

Helpful Tips and Lessons Learned

Twenty years from now you will be more disappointed by the things you didn't do than by the ones you did do. So, throw off the bowlines. Sail away from the safe harbor. Catch the trade winds in your sails.
Explore. Dream. Discover. –Mark Twain

Lots of things can ruin an otherwise fine outing, and many of them you can't really anticipate in advance, or do anything about. A lose rock can cause a twisted ankle, an unpredicted snowstorm can obscure a trail, or a fellow hiker may become ill. Thomas Jefferson once said, *"I am a great believer in luck, and I find that the harder I work, the more I have of it."* The same can be said for hiking or rafting the Grand Canyon. Careful planning and research, attention to the smallest details, and being prepared for the worst, while hoping for the best, can weight luck in your favor.

After a lifetime of hiking, I have learned a lot about the gear I've used-and abused. This chapter provides some of these insights, as well as specific recommendations for certain equipment I have the highest, trail-tested confidence in.

Footwear

Your feet are the foundation of a successful, or unsuccessful, hike. If you are new to hiking, or looking to upgrade your equipment, a good pair of trail shoes or boots should be in your future. Over the past few decades, as the sport of hiking has boomed, so has the specialization of footwear. Today, hikers are faced with many confusing choices: high-cut or low-cut, flexible or stiff midsoles, crampon attachable, breathable or waterproof, fabric or leather, deep lugs or sticky rubber soles, suede or smooth leather, removable insole, glued or stitched, rubber rand, gusseted tongue, padded upper collar, etc.

My advice is to purchase footwear from a reputable company, and try on several different styles before making a purchase. I had my share of trial-and-error before I finally found the perfect boots for me. Since I often make lengthy hikes with a heavy backpack, I selected the Vasque Sundowner smooth leather boot, and have never regretted my decision. I have a U.S. size 10½ foot but wear a size 12 boot to allow plenty of extra toe room. My first pair of Sundowners lasted 9-10 years until I needed to have them re-soled. I sent them to a boot repair company in Boulder, Colorado, and they came back looking nearly as good as new. Another couple thousand miles later I needed a second re-sole.

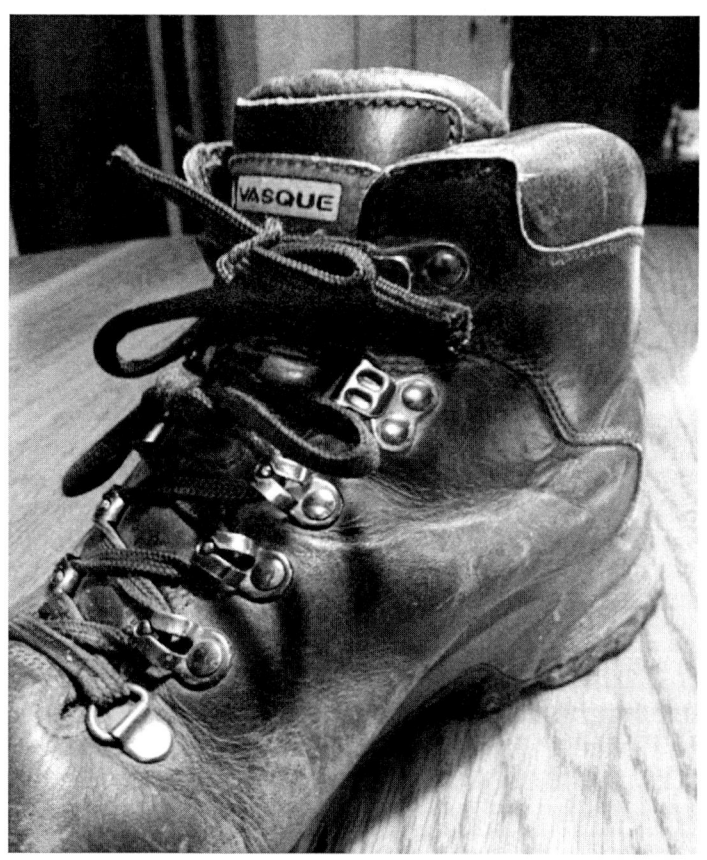

My Well-Worn Vasque Sundowner Boots, Double-Tied in "Downhill Mode."

Once again, the boots cleaned up nicely under professional care, and the new soles lasted me many more years. Eventually, the upper leather wore out and I purchased a new pair of Sundowners. I have had my latest pair for 13 years and they are still going strong.

One great product that helps keep my boot leather in good shape is Nikwax Waterproofing Wax. About twice a year, and always before a wet or snowy hike, I apply a couple of coats of Nikwax with my bare hands. It's a U.K. product widely available in the U.S. as a cream in a squeeze tube, and it never disappoints.

During a remote hike on the Tanner to New Hance route, I met three guys who were on a week-long excursion. As we sat on a beach near Nevills Rapids and shared morning snacks and stories, I noticed he had a unique way of lacing up his hiking boots. I tried, and then adopted, his method of "double tying" the laces for flat or downhill hiking (not uphill), and I've never had a blackened toenail or blister since then. For high-cut boots like I have, I now make a double knot at the mid-point of my boot tongue, and tie another double knot at the top of the tongue (see picture). The boot laces held by the lower knot are pulled tightly so that my foot won't slip forward while hiking downhill. The remainder of the lacing to the top of the boot is tied at a normal tightness to provide good ankle support. Another advantage to this method is that my boot laces aren't long enough to accidently trip on.

Socks

Good boots with inadequate socks will still give you problems. As you might guess, there's a large variety of socks on the market these days: Merino wool (nylon, spandex and Lycra blend), SmartWool (wool, nylon and elastic blend), and PrimaLoft (polyester, merino wool, nylon and Lycra blend) are all popular materials.

I have two favorite socks; one for winter hiking and one for the rest of the year. My favorite winter sock is the very well-padded Thorlo TKX. When hiking with crampons or snowshoes, they insulate from the cold, wick moisture away from my feet, and never lose their shape or "ball-up" when wet. My favorite three season sock is the SmartWool PhD. They work best without any type of liner, dry quickly, and provide the snug fit I need since my hiking boots are intentionally larger than other shoes I wear.

Pants

While your choice of hiking pants is certainly not as critical as your choice of shoes or socks, there are certain things I have learned to look for which guide my purchases. Hiking pants should be light weight, wind, water and abrasion resistant, dry quickly, have useful pockets-including at least one with a zippered opening, use nylon vs. metal zippers, and have numerous belt loops large enough for nylon belts.

After many years of mediocre pants, I finally found all of these features, and more, in my North Face convertible pants. Grand Canyon hiking can involve large temperature extremes. In the winter, the temperature at the South Rim is often below freezing. However, if I'm hiking to the bottom of the canyon, it can quickly warm to 70 degrees or more. In winter, I wear medium weight Patagonia Capilene long underwear as a base layer, and wear my North Face convertibles as the outer shell. As I hike down into warmer weather, I zip-off the bottom half of my pants and quickly turn them into shorts.

Shirts

In warm weather, which is usually the case in Arizona, I prefer to hike in light-colored, cotton T-shirts. Cotton is breathable and absorbs water and sweat, which makes it an ideal choice when the weather is warm or hot. I don't care for shirts that wick away moisture in the summer for one simple reason–moisture is nature's way of keeping us cool.

Winter weather hiking is all about layering. In winter, moisture is your enemy. Dry and warm is your friend. Wicking fabrics that move moisture *away* from your skin are an essential base layer. I've found that most long-sleeved, synthetic fabric shirts work well. Be sure to also wear a middle insulating layer, and follow this with an outer layer of waterproof and windproof material.

Hats

The humble hat is one of your most important outdoor recreation items. The legend that we lose most of our body heat through our head is not true. However, it is true that the head contains many blood vessels that are close to the skin. In cold weather, without an insulating hat or stocking cap, the blood flowing through your scalp will be cooled as it returns to your warmer body. The head makes up 7% to 9% of the body's surface area, and can result in 10% heat loss in cold weather if not properly protected.[1]

Since I hike mostly in Arizona, and in the severe sun, I always wear a wide-brimmed hat. My Dorfman Pacific Solar Weave mesh hat is 100% cotton, and has breathable mesh between the top and the wide brim. It also has a chin strap so that it doesn't blow away if I am on a river trip. In the heat of the summer, I pour water on the inside or dip it in a stream. It also has a flexible brim so that the back of the hat doesn't come in contact with my backpack frame. It's a three-season hat that works great for me.

For winter hikes, I usually wear a simple, North Face beanie made from Polartec. It's inexpensive, blocks the cold and wind, and weighs next to nothing. For extreme weather I wear a SmartWool balaclava, and also glacier glasses with side shields for full protection of my head and eyes. This outfit makes me look like a bank robber, but at least I'm warm!

Underwear

While not a glamorous subject like boots, the wrong underwear on a lengthy trip can be a real pain in the butt…so to speak. Moisture wicking underwear, whether worn in winter or summer, is the way to go. I like ExOfficio Give-N-Go boxers for hiking and for river trips. They stretch but retain their shape, are quick drying, and are quite comfortable. Avoid cotton at all cost.

Writing a book about my hiking experiences has had the benefit of reminding me of many helpful tips, and some valuable lessons, that I've either been taught by others or have learned on my own. Here, are some things that might help you have a good hike or river trip:

Uphill hikers always have the right-of-way.

Purchase hiking shoes or boots that are at least one size larger than you normally wear.

Cotton balls in the toes of your hiking boots will help cushion your toes and nails if your boots are too small.

Cut your toenails 3-4 days before your hike.

Bring a small amount of duck tape wrapped around a hiking stick or a small prescription bottle. Put a small piece of tape on any "hot spots" on your feet or toes before they develop into blisters.

Bring some lightweight flip flops for when you are in camp. Inexpensive ones usually don't cost too much and are lightweight.

Apply a liberal amount of powder to your feet, and to the inside of your boots, each morning.

When you stop to rest, elevate your feet. It will send more blood to your legs, which helps to reduce the lactic acid that builds up in your muscles.

Drink at least a pint of water or electrolyte-enhanced fluid before you begin your hike. Your stomach is a canteen, too. If you aren't peeing at least once an hour, you are not drinking enough.

Wear a hat in the winter and in the summer.

For multi-day backpacking trips, organize your pack with Ziplok freezer bags: Label them Kitchen, Bathroom, First Aid, Medicines, etc. This will help keep your things both organized and dry.

Bring a small package of wet wipes. They are great for cleaning most anything.

Bring a few Zip Ties. They work wonders for mending tears or breaks.

If you're going on a river trip, bring ankle-high socks to wear with your river sandals. The socks will eliminate painful abrasion from sand that will get between your feet and the sandal straps.

Stuff your tent and ground cloth into their stuff sack rather than folding them. Repeated folding tends to wear out the thin layer of seam seal and leads to leaks.

Apples and bagels pack really well and last for several days. So does a low moisture cheese like Gouda.

Surprisingly, pre-packaged salads can last quite a while. Wrap them in clothes, put them deep in your pack, and enjoy them for several days.

Place some dehydrated fruit (apples, apricots, raisins, cranberries, etc.) into a cup or pot of cool water before going to bed. In the morning they will be fully hydrated and great to mix into instant oatmeal.

An empty plastic bladder from a wine box makes a great small, weightless pillow. Simply open the wine spigot, blow as much air as you want into it, and wrap a shirt around it. You have an instant pillow.

Always keep a cotton bandana in your pocket. They are great for cleaning glasses, wiping your brow, shading your neck, as a mask for blowing dust, pre-filtering water, making a sweatband, stabilizing a sprained ankle, washing or drying yourself, or covering food. You can even use them to blow your nose!

Closing Thoughts

Physical preparation is critical for successful Grand Canyon hiking. Since I had an office job most of my life, one way I prepared for the extensive downhill hiking was to sit in my office chair, lift my legs out straight, and hold them there as long as possible-often for 10 minutes at a time. This simple exercise strengthens the quads, which are your "brakes" as you hike down into the canyon, and your "engines" when you hike back out.

Remember that you are hiking to see and experience new things…not just new foods and equipment. Put your emphasis on what you are seeing and where you are, and not on the equipment and meals. Bring easily prepared foods, or freeze-dried meals. Most of them taste pretty good, come in a wide variety, and pack sufficient, dense calories. Remember, it's not about what you take into the canyon-it's what you experience, remember, and take back out with you.

Finally, take time to consider the small things. Smell the wet bank of the river, feel the slight evening breeze as the canyon begins to cool down, look for ancient fossils in the limestone, watch the sun come up over the high canyon walls, keep an eye out for petroglyphs and pictographs left by those who lived here long ago, and gaze at the dark, star-filled sky from your cot or sleeping bag. You are in an amazing place and, like a true friend, it gets better and more intimate the more you learn and listen as it quietly speaks to you.

1. www.bbc.com/future/story/20130708-is-most-heat-loss-from-your-head

EPILOGUE

It took me nearly a year to write this book, idle times included, and I enjoyed every moment of it. I particularly enjoyed learning the unique history behind some of my favorite places. At one point in my writing, I had reached a dead end and was searching for inspiration. I decided I needed to visit, and write, at the Grand Canyon.

On a cool, spring day, laptop and lunch in-hand, my wife and I hiked the short seldom visited trail to Shoshone Point, a stunning and expansive viewpoint on the South Rim. I had set up shop, and was thinking about what to write, when we noticed two middle-aged women walking, purses and camera in hand, to the very rim of the Canyon. They were having difficulty descending the uneven rock ledges toward the edge. We decided to see if they needed any help. I approached the first woman and struck up a conversation. She kindly replied that they were from the Midwest, and she was accompanying her good friend who was on a sad journey with her daughter. When I inquired where her friend's daughter was, she tearfully replied, "She's in my friend's purse." I was stunned and uncharacteristically speechless. It took me a moment to process what she had said. The woman went on to tell me that her friend's daughter had been killed in a car accident. She had always loved the Grand Canyon, and her mother was quietly and privately fulfilling her wishes. That day, at the moment when I witnessed a grief-stricken mother scattering her daughter's ashes to the winds, I found the inspiration I had been seeking. A gift from a grieving stranger.

Nearly thirty years ago I had a business colleague from Canada visiting me in Phoenix for several days of meetings. He had no weekend plans, so I invited him to join my daughter and me for a day trip to the Grand Canyon. He readily agreed, and excitedly said it had been a life-long dream of his to see it. We parked at the first viewing area, Mather Point, and I told my friend to close his eyes. My daughter took him by the arm and led him to the guardrail at the edge of the canyon. When she told him to open his eyes, he stared for several moments and then wept. He later told me that he had been overwhelmed by what he was seeing. He'd never known anything like it, and it was confusing, frightening, and wonderful at the same time. We walked part way down the Bright Angel Trail, and he later told me it had been one of the best days of his life.

Perhaps I take it for granted. I sure hope not. Maybe I've been there so many times that it's no longer as impressive to me as it deserves to be. On the other hand, when I first begin a hike into the canyon I feel as if I'm coming home to somewhere I've known for a very long time. Like my grandma's welcoming kitchen that always looked, smelled, and felt the same each time I walked through that squeaky screen door in Indiana.

When I was on the slow, uneven road to recovery after my problematic gallbladder surgery, I told my wife I wanted to visit the Grand Canyon. Not to hike, just to be there, at my church. I was still on several strong medications, so she drove while I watched out the window. There wasn't much I could do once we arrived, but we enjoyed a nice sunset and dinner at the El Tovar. By morning, I knew exactly what I wanted to do. We took the shuttle to the Shrine of the Ages, and walked from there to the Grand Canyon Pioneer Cemetery. Not your typical tourist attraction, but extremely interesting to us. We saw the final resting places of famous pioneers such as Bill Bass, Ralph Cameron, John Hance, Emery and Ellsworth Kolb, John Verkamp, Gunner Widforss, several Harvey Girls, and a memorial to the victims of the worst air disaster of its time over the Grand Canyon. It was good to be back at the canyon, and I was exceedingly happy that I was only visiting, and not *in* the cemetery.

Today, my wife and I enjoy a very active life in retirement. We both left our jobs early in life, and with plenty of tread left on our hiking boots. I am learning how to be a volunteer first responder in our local community, and we explore new trails and streams almost every week. Our love of the Grand Canyon is as strong as ever. It seems the more we see, the more we realize there is still so much more to be explored.

Sincere thanks and appreciation go out to you, my readers, for your interest in the Grand Canyon. If you haven't visited yet, I hope you have the opportunity. Mother Nature, in all of her resplendence, awaits you.

> *I went to the woods because I wished to live deliberately,*
> *to front only the essential facts of life,*
> *and see if I could learn what it had to teach,*
> *and not, when I came to die, discover that I had not lived.*
> -Henry David Thoreau

My desk at Shoshoni Point. Courtesy of National Park Service.

Field Notes

Field Notes

Field Notes